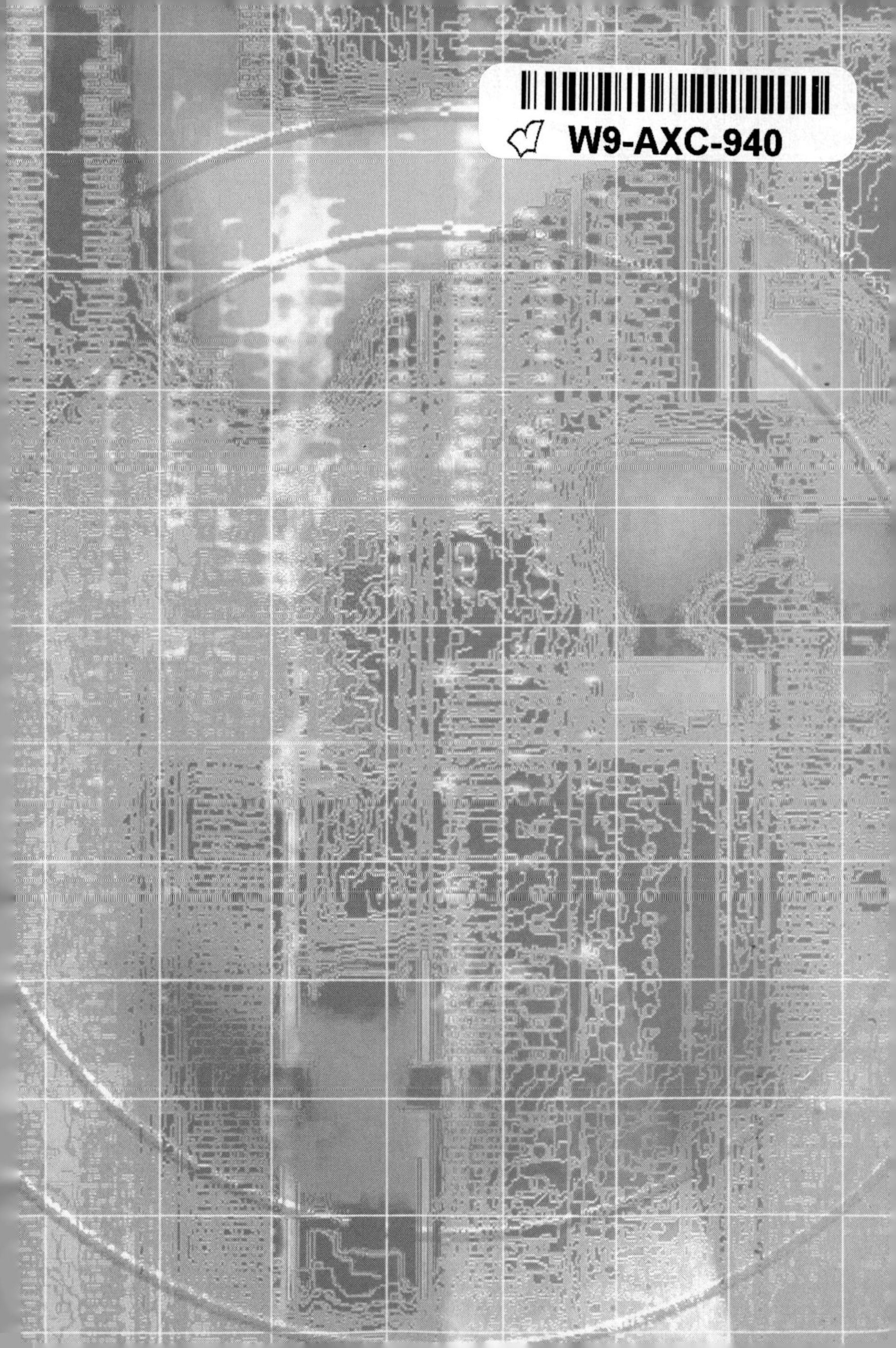

Chaotic Century
Volume 03

Story and Art by **MICHIRO UEYAMA**

English Adaptation & Editing: William Flanagan
Translator: Kaori Kawakubo Inoue
Touch-up & Lettering: Dan Nakrosis
Graphics, Design & Zoids Guru: Benjamin Wright

Managing Editor: Annette Roman
VP of Sales & Marketing: Rick Bauer
Editor-in-Chief: Hyoe Narita
Publisher: Seiji Horibuchi

Printed in Canada.

Published by Viz Comics
P.O. Box 77010 • San Francisco, CA 94107

10 9 8 7 6 5 4 3 2 1
First printing, April 2002

Call us toll free at
(800) 394-3042 and
ask for your **FREE** Viz
Shop-By-Mail catalog!

WHY IS IT BACKWARDS?

ZOIDS was originally a Japanese comic (manga), and since
the Japanese read right-to-left, the comic you're reading is a
mirror image of the original drawings. So if you noticed that
the mark on Van's face is on the wrong side, that's why.

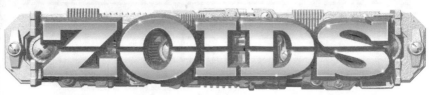

Chaotic Century

Story and Art by
MICHIRO UEYAMA

Planet Zi orbits a sun sixty thousand light years from our Earth on the opposite side of galactic center. There, countless varieties of giant life forms with metal-based bodies—ZOIDS—inhabit the world. The people of Zi took those lifeforms and altered them into beastly fighting machines, and the wars spread throughout the planet. When humans from Earth arrived in an enormous life-ship, they added their advanced technology to the warlike atmosphere causing a ZOID arms race.

Some 40 years ago, a gigantic meteorite collided with Zi. Millions were killed and a large portion of a continent was sunk beneath the waves. The strike caused cataclysmic earthquakes and volcanic eruptions—much of Zi's history was buried beneath lava and dust. Now, in the remote region of the Elemia Desert, young Van finds a small dinosaur-type ZOID while searching a ruin. The ZOID, Zeke, can merge with Van and also merge with other ZOIDS, boosting their power and combat abilities. Beside the capsule from which Zeke emerged, Van finds another capsule that contains a strange young woman with a telepathic connection to Zeke as well as with other ZOIDS. She remembers that her name is Fiona, but nothing beyond that.

Van and Zeke successfully protect the village from a ZOID-hating pilot, Raven, but buildings are destroyed and the villagers suffer many losses. Van must make a decision: to stay in the village—the only life he has ever known—or venture into the world to discover the mysteries behind the origin of Zeke and Fiona...

The Desert Cyclone

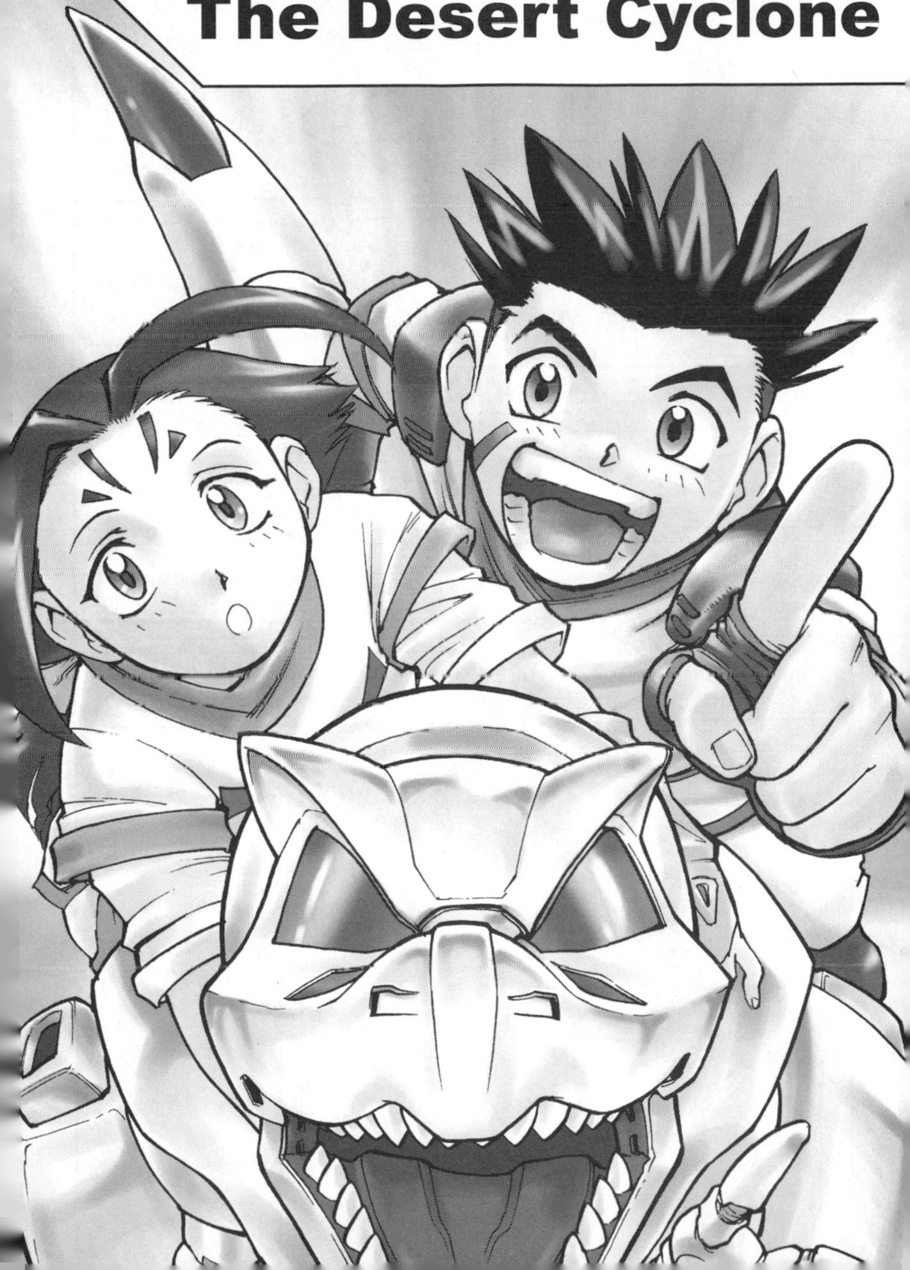

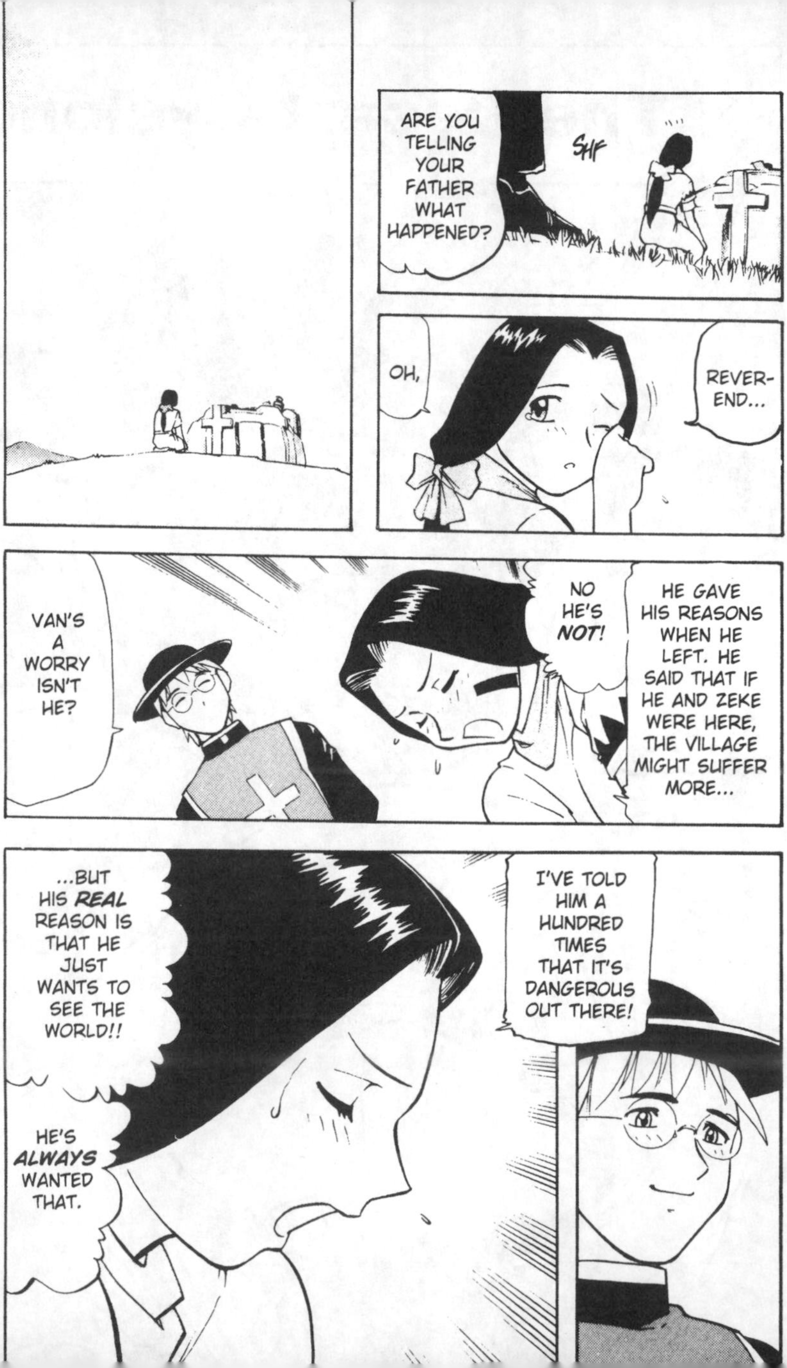
ARE YOU TELLING YOUR FATHER WHAT HAPPENED?
SHF
OH,
REVER-END...
VAN'S A WORRY ISN'T HE?
NO HE'S *NOT*!
HE GAVE HIS REASONS WHEN HE LEFT. HE SAID THAT IF HE AND ZEKE WERE HERE, THE VILLAGE MIGHT SUFFER MORE...
...BUT HIS *REAL* REASON IS THAT HE JUST WANTS TO SEE THE WORLD!!
HE'S *ALWAYS* WANTED THAT.
I'VE TOLD HIM A HUNDRED TIMES THAT IT'S DANGEROUS OUT THERE!

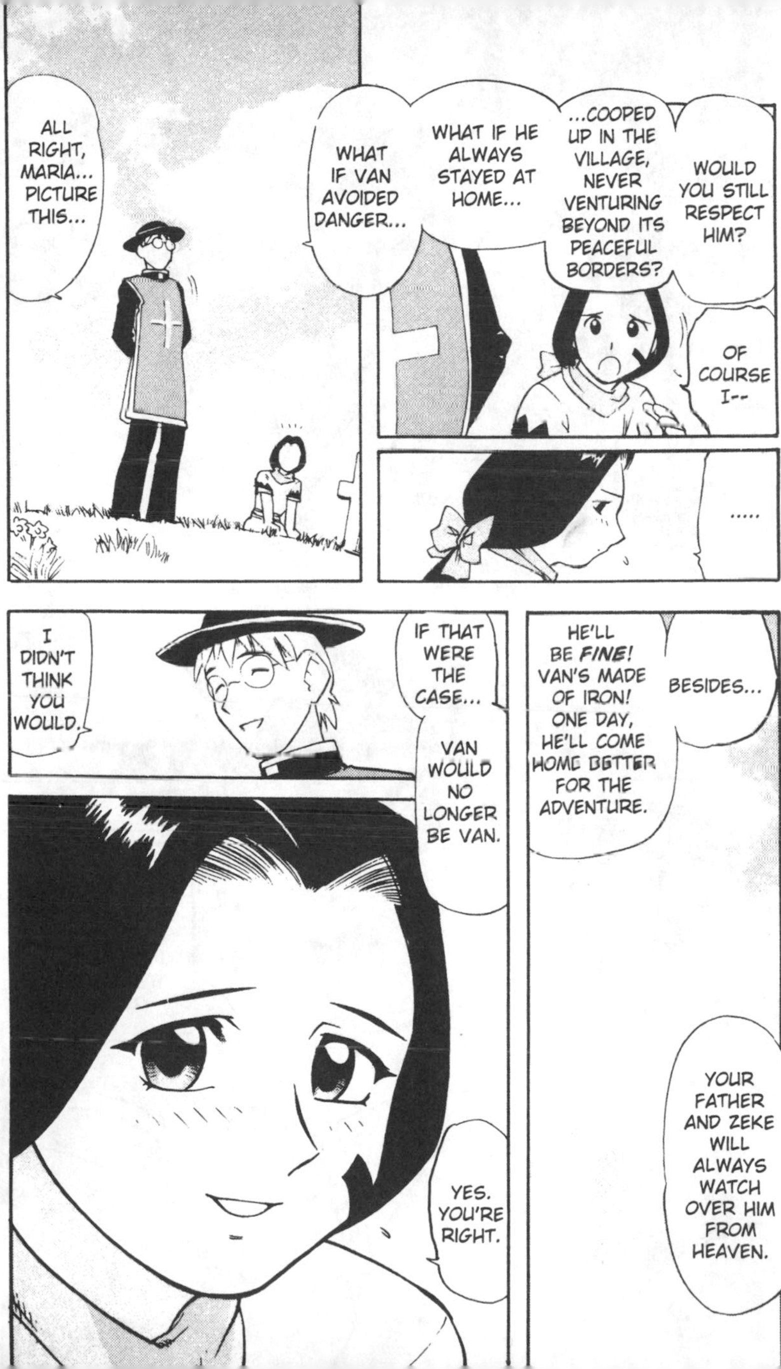
ALL RIGHT, MARIA... PICTURE THIS...
WHAT IF VAN AVOIDED DANGER...
WHAT IF HE ALWAYS STAYED AT HOME...
...COOPED UP IN THE VILLAGE, NEVER VENTURING BEYOND ITS PEACEFUL BORDERS?
WOULD YOU STILL RESPECT HIM?
OF COURSE I--
.....
I DIDN'T THINK YOU WOULD.
IF THAT WERE THE CASE...
VAN WOULD NO LONGER BE VAN.
HE'LL BE *FINE*! VAN'S MADE OF IRON! ONE DAY, HE'LL COME HOME BETTER FOR THE ADVENTURE.
BESIDES...
YES. YOU'RE RIGHT.
YOUR FATHER AND ZEKE WILL ALWAYS WATCH OVER HIM FROM HEAVEN.

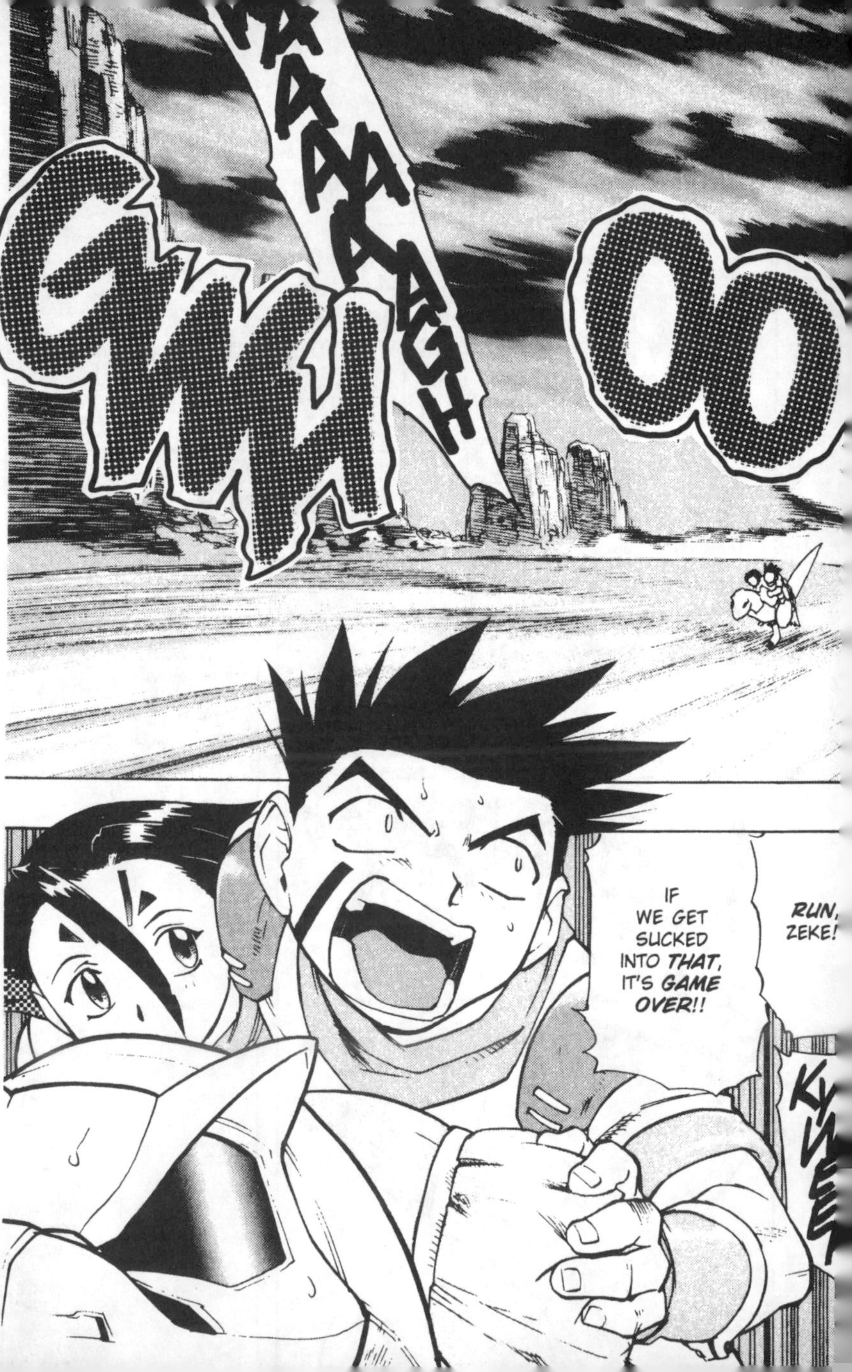
AAAAAAGH
GWU
OO
IF WE GET SUCKED INTO *THAT*, IT'S ***GAME OVER!!***
RUN, ZEKE!
KYUEE

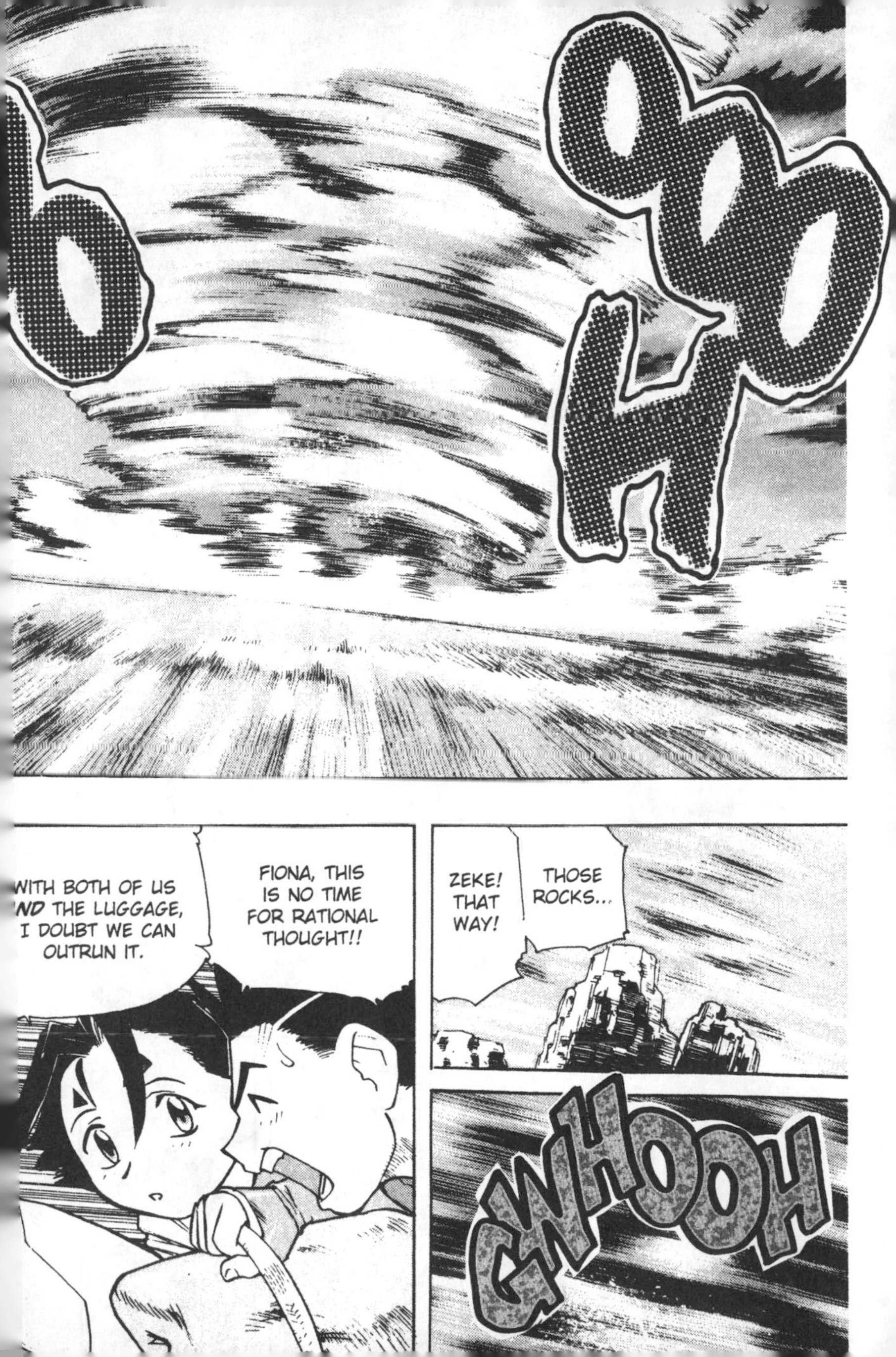
WITH BOTH OF US ND THE LUGGAGE, I DOUBT WE CAN OUTRUN IT.
FIONA, THIS IS NO TIME FOR RATIONAL THOUGHT!!
ZEKE! THAT WAY!
THOSE ROCKS...
GWHOOH

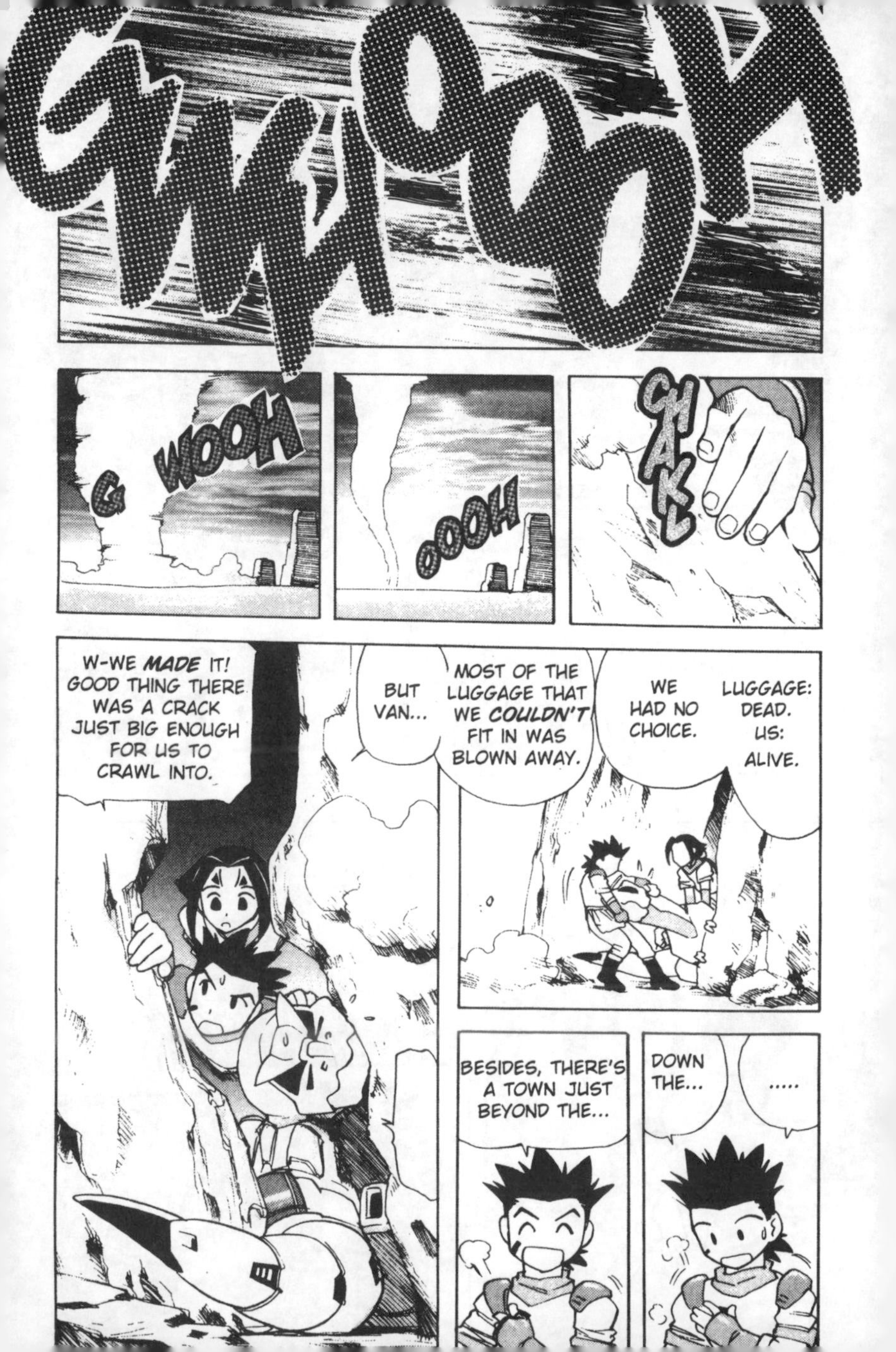
GWOOOOOH
G WOOH
OOOH
CHAKL
W-WE *MADE* IT! GOOD THING THERE WAS A CRACK JUST BIG ENOUGH FOR US TO CRAWL INTO.
BUT VAN...
MOST OF THE LUGGAGE THAT WE *COULDN'T* FIT IN WAS BLOWN AWAY.
WE HAD NO CHOICE.
LUGGAGE: DEAD. US: ALIVE.
BESIDES, THERE'S A TOWN JUST BEYOND THE...
DOWN THE...
.....

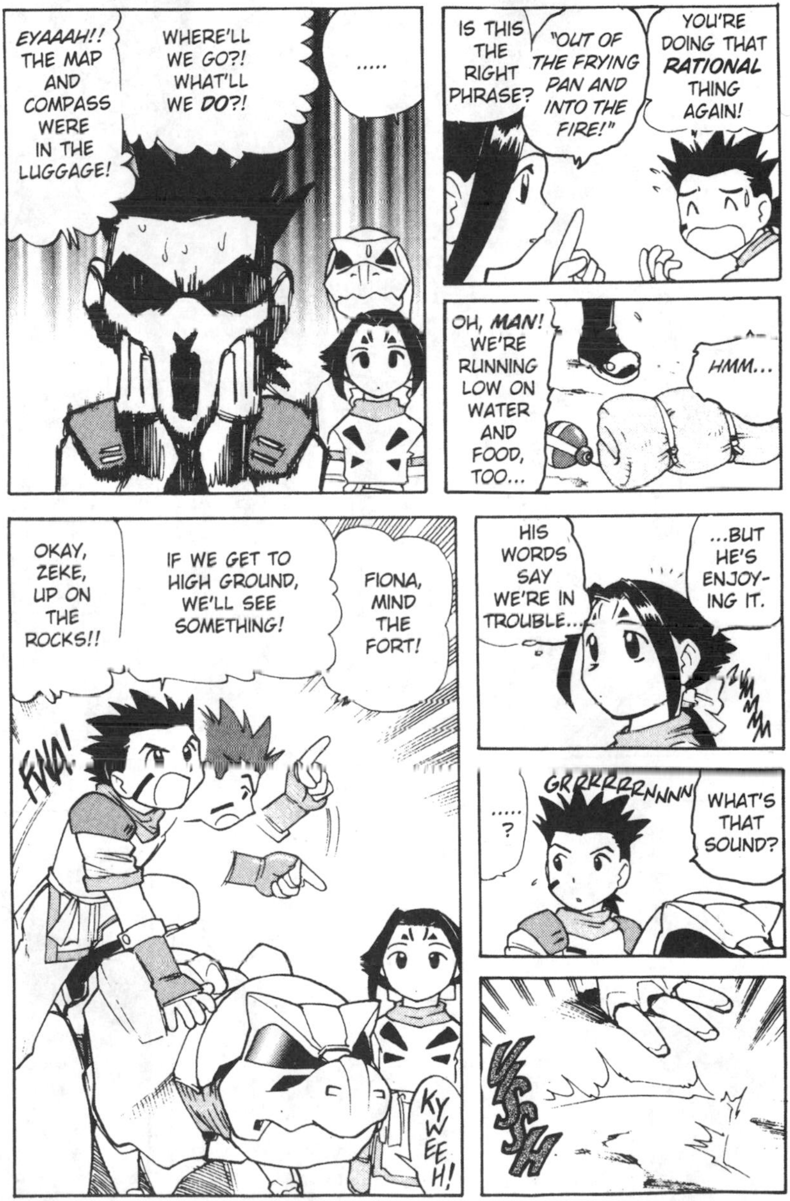
EYAAAH!! THE MAP AND COMPASS WERE IN THE LUGGAGE!
WHERE'LL WE GO?! WHAT'LL WE DO?!
.....
IS THIS THE RIGHT PHRASE?
"OUT OF THE FRYING PAN AND INTO THE FIRE!"
YOU'RE DOING THAT RATIONAL THING AGAIN!
OH, MAN! WE'RE RUNNING LOW ON WATER AND FOOD, TOO...
HMM...
OKAY, ZEKE, UP ON THE ROCKS!!
IF WE GET TO HIGH GROUND, WE'LL SEE SOMETHING!
FIONA, MIND THE FORT!
KYWEEH!
HIS WORDS SAY WE'RE IN TROUBLE...
...BUT HE'S ENJOYING IT.
.....?
GRRRRRRNNNN
WHAT'S THAT SOUND?
VSSH

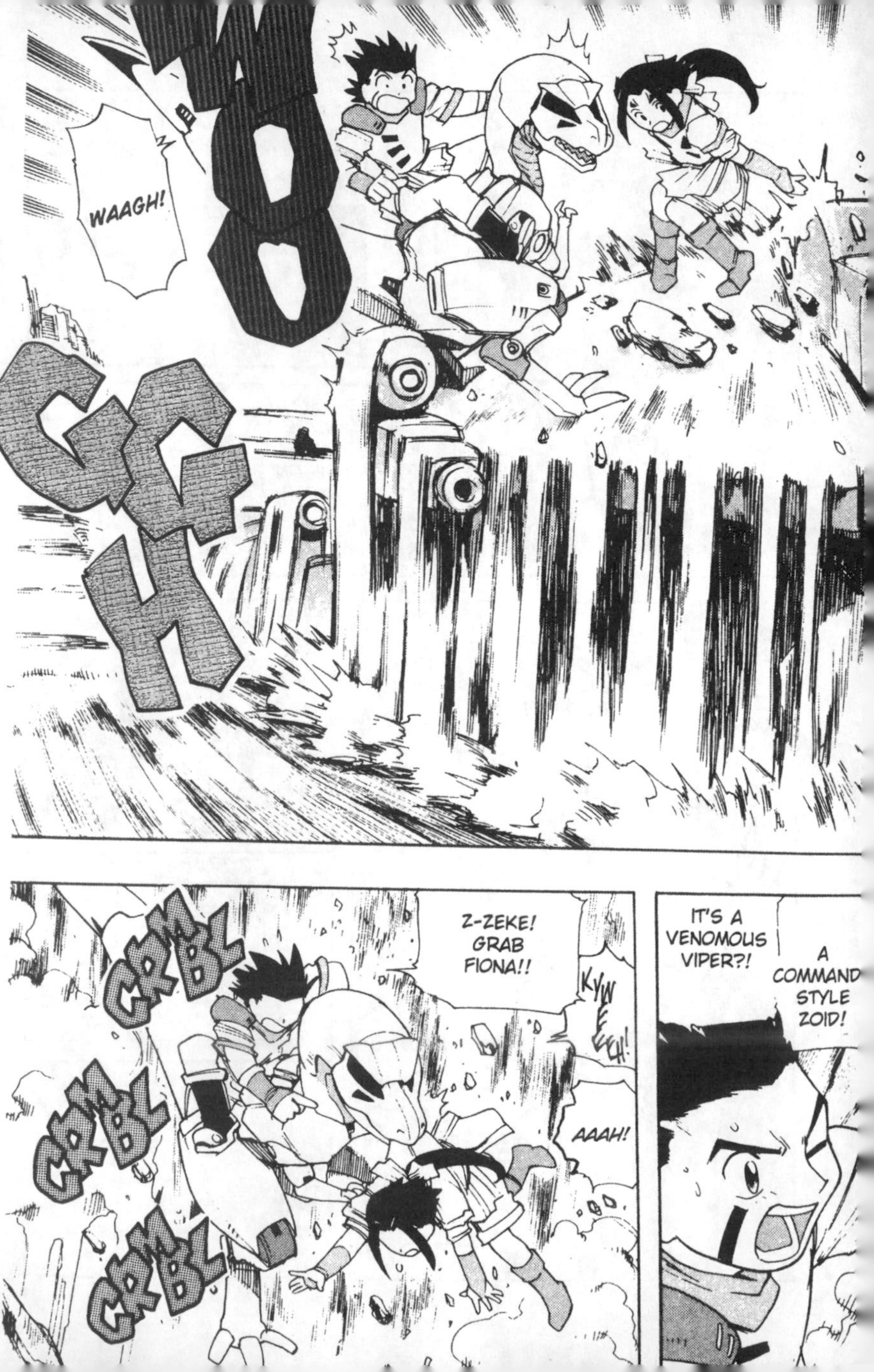
WAAGH!
CRMBL
CRMBL
CRMBL
Z-ZEKE! GRAB FIONA!!
KYWEECH!
AAAH!
IT'S A VENOMOUS VIPER?!
A COMMAND STYLE ZOID!

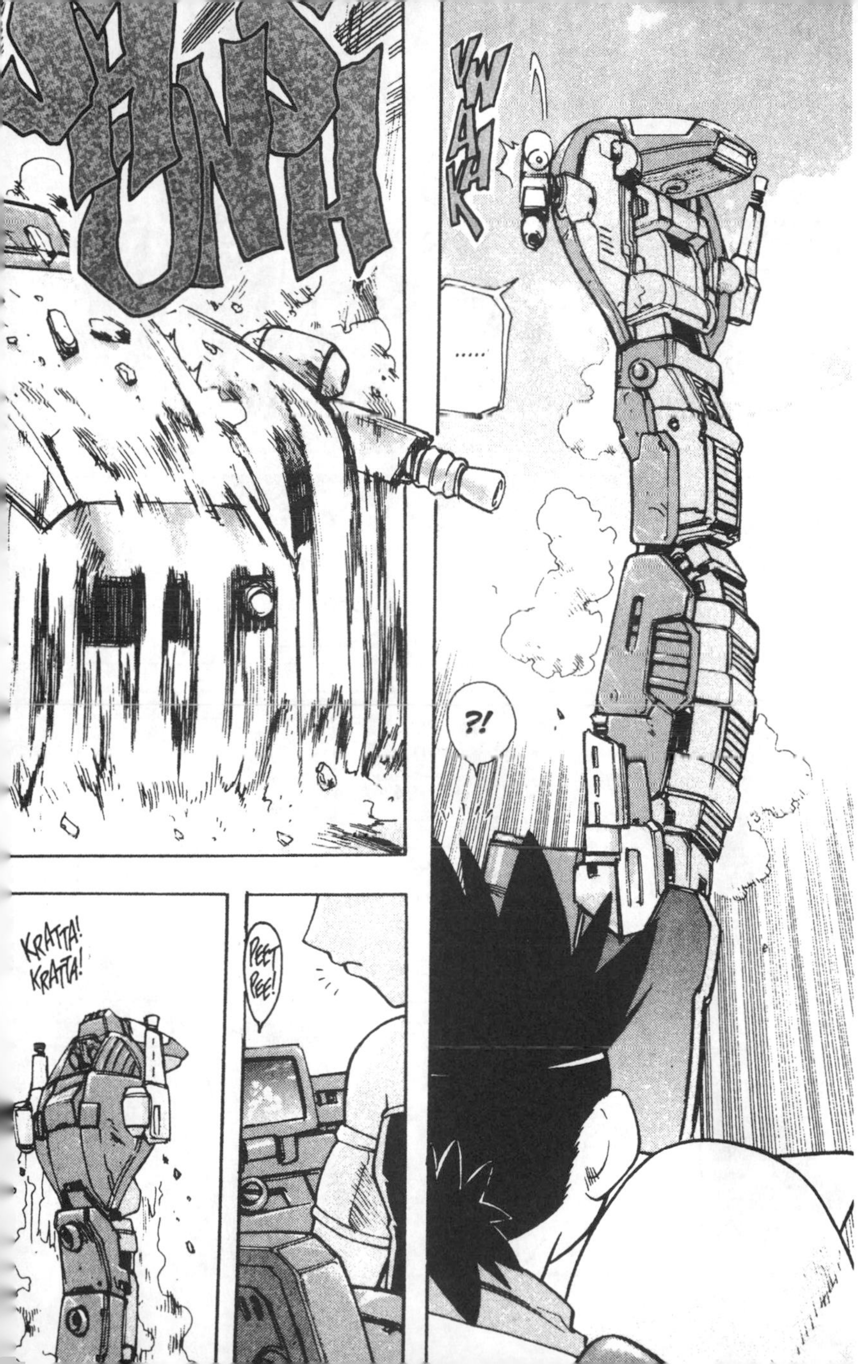
CRUNCH
KRATTA! KRATTA!
PEEP PEE!
VWAKK
......
?!

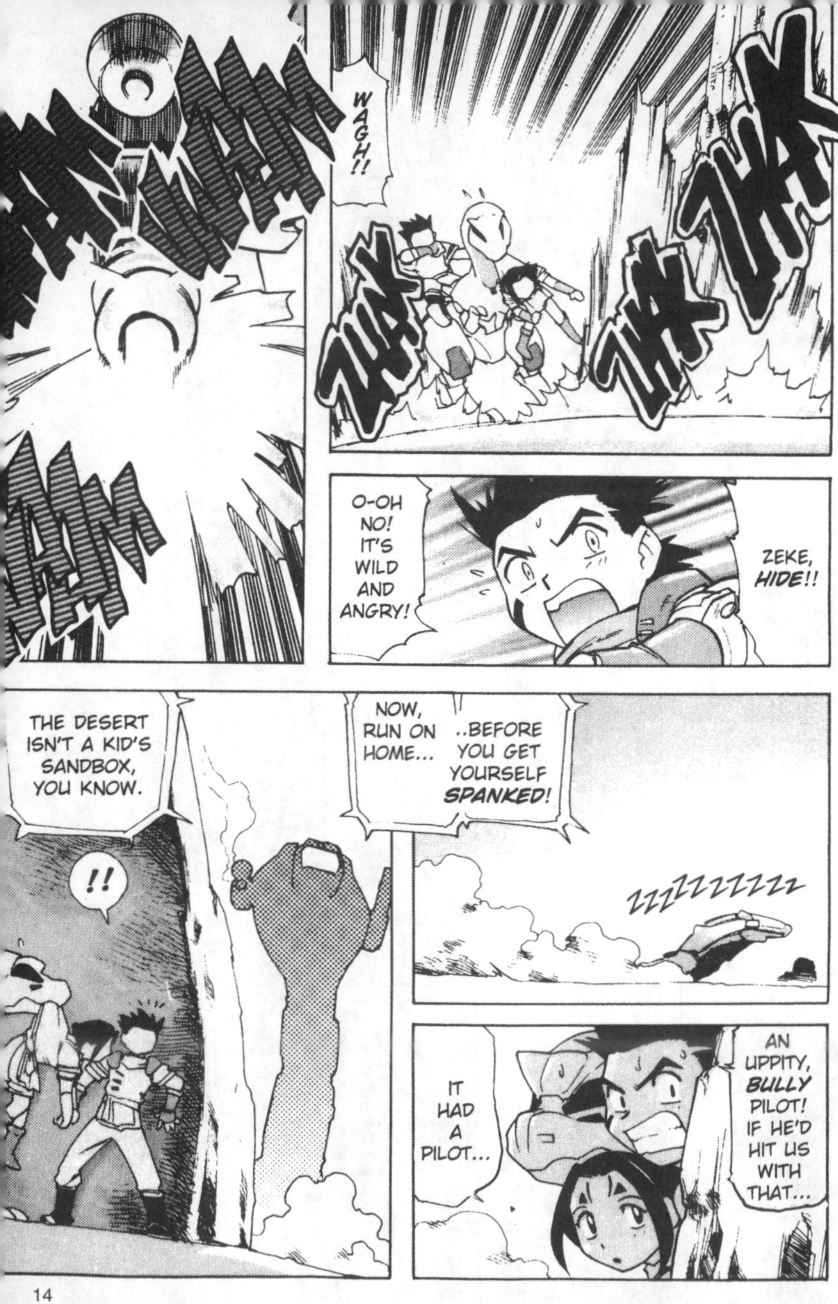
WAGH!!
O-OH NO! IT'S WILD AND ANGRY!
ZEKE, HIDE!!
THE DESERT ISN'T A KID'S SANDBOX, YOU KNOW.
NOW, RUN ON HOME...
!!
..BEFORE YOU GET YOURSELF SPANKED!
ZZZZZZZZZZ
IT HAD A PILOT...
AN UPPITY, BULLY PILOT! IF HE'D HIT US WITH THAT...

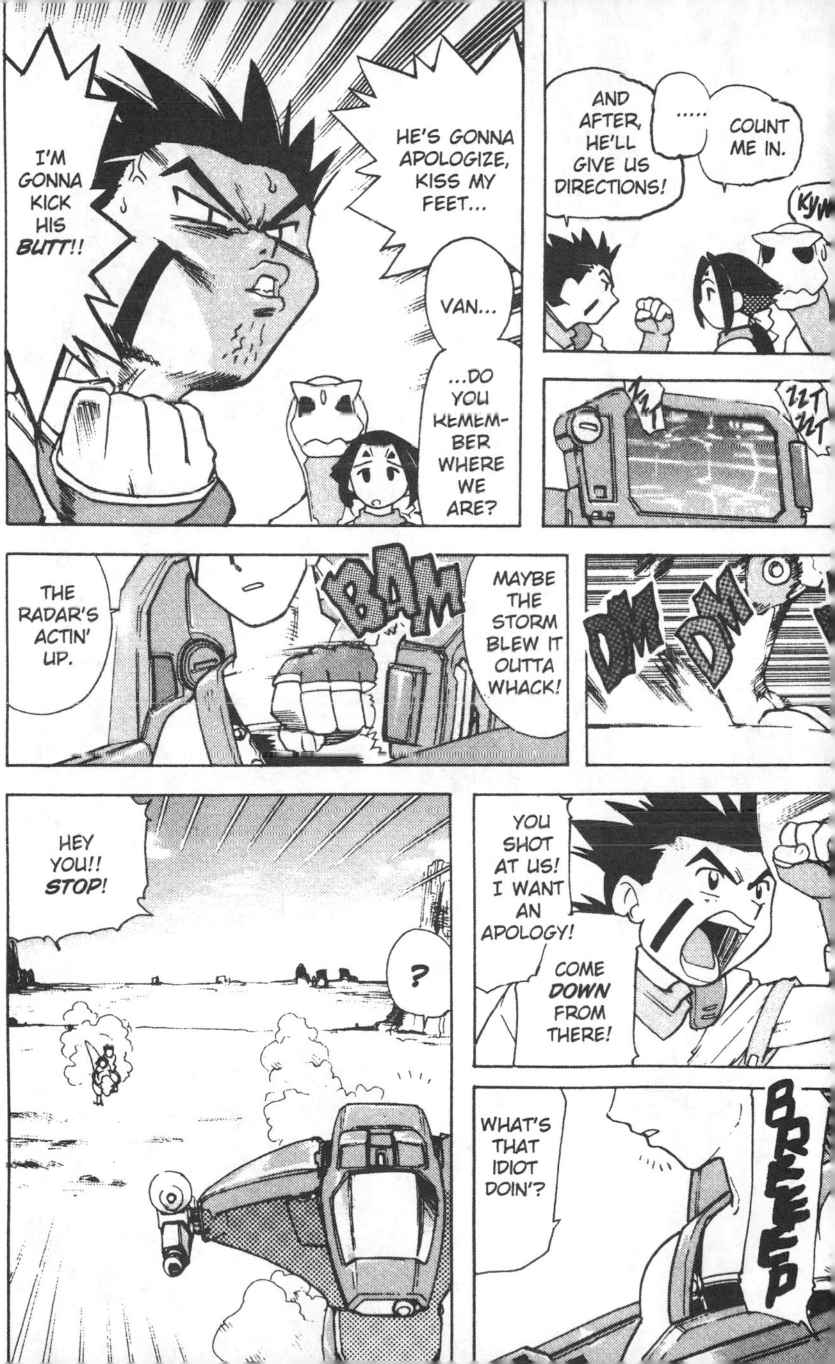
I'M GONNA KICK HIS *BUTT*!!
HE'S GONNA APOLOGIZE, KISS MY FEET...
VAN...
...DO YOU REMEMBER WHERE WE ARE?
AND AFTER, HE'LL GIVE US DIRECTIONS!
.....
COUNT ME IN.
ZZT
ZZT
ZZT
THE RADAR'S ACTIN' UP.
BAM
MAYBE THE STORM BLEW IT OUTTA WHACK!
DM
DM
HEY YOU!! *STOP*!
?
YOU SHOT AT US! I WANT AN APOLOGY!
COME *DOWN* FROM THERE!
WHAT'S THAT IDIOT DOIN'?
BREEEP

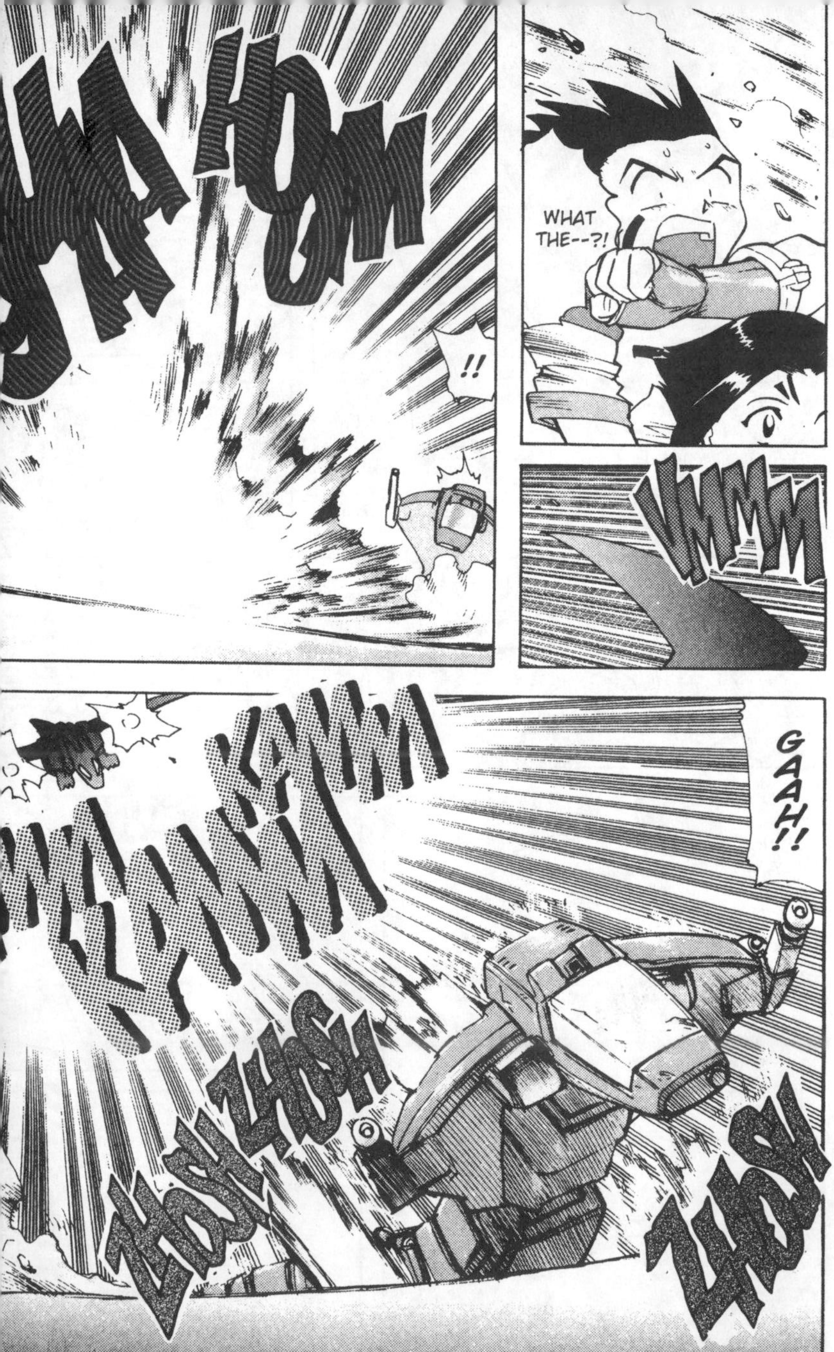
!!
WHAT THE--?!
VMMM
ZHOSH ZHOSH
GAAH!!
ZHOSH

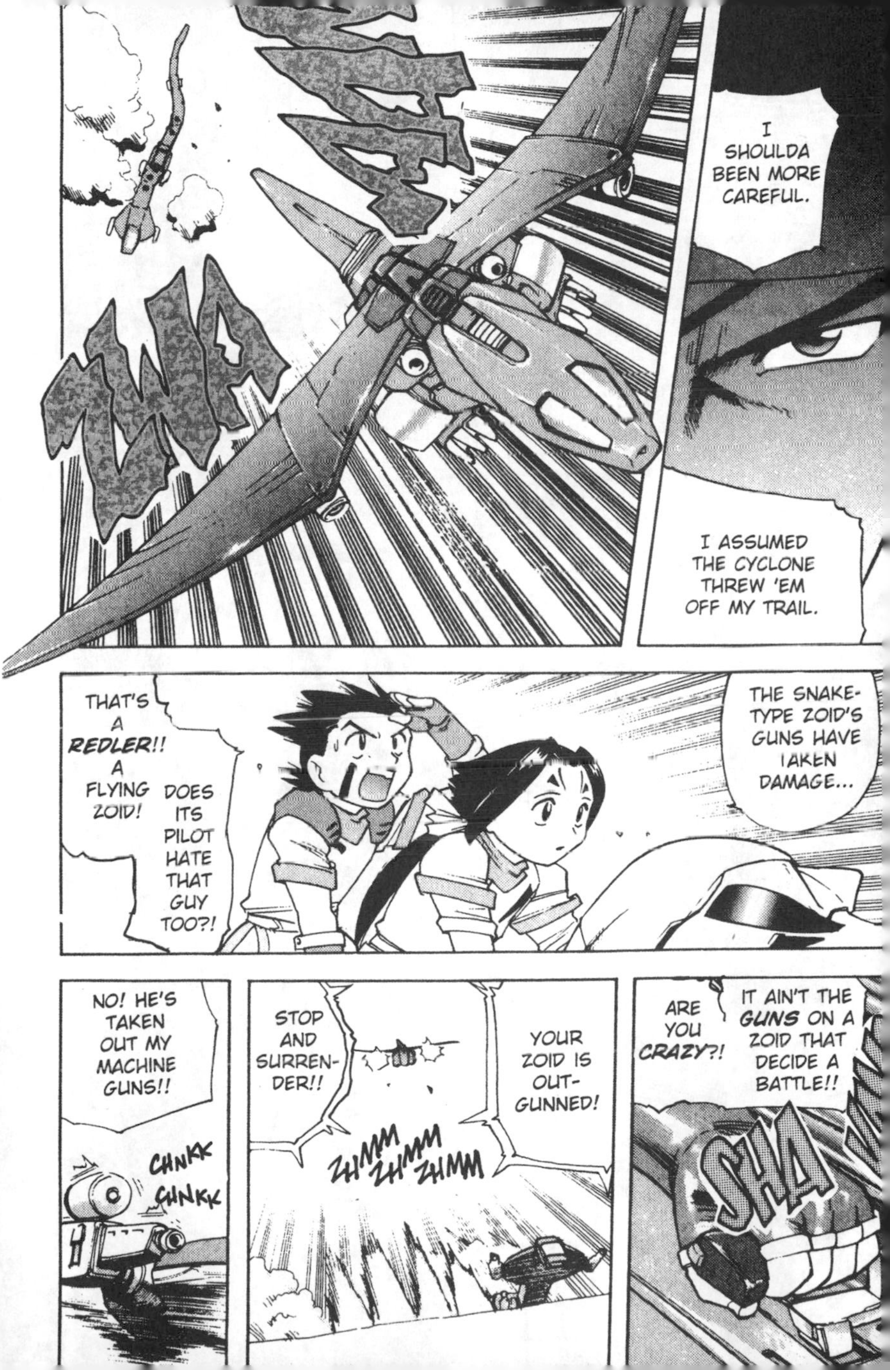
ZWA
ZWA
I SHOULDA BEEN MORE CAREFUL.
I ASSUMED THE CYCLONE THREW 'EM OFF MY TRAIL.
THAT'S A **REDLER**!! A FLYING ZOID!
DOES ITS PILOT HATE THAT GUY TOO?!
THE SNAKE-TYPE ZOID'S GUNS HAVE TAKEN DAMAGE...
NO! HE'S TAKEN OUT MY MACHINE GUNS!!
CHNKK
CHNKK
STOP AND SURREN-DER!!
YOUR ZOID IS OUT-GUNNED!
ZHMM ZHMM ZHMM
ARE YOU **CRAZY**?!
IT AIN'T THE **GUNS** ON A ZOID THAT DECIDE A BATTLE!!
SHA

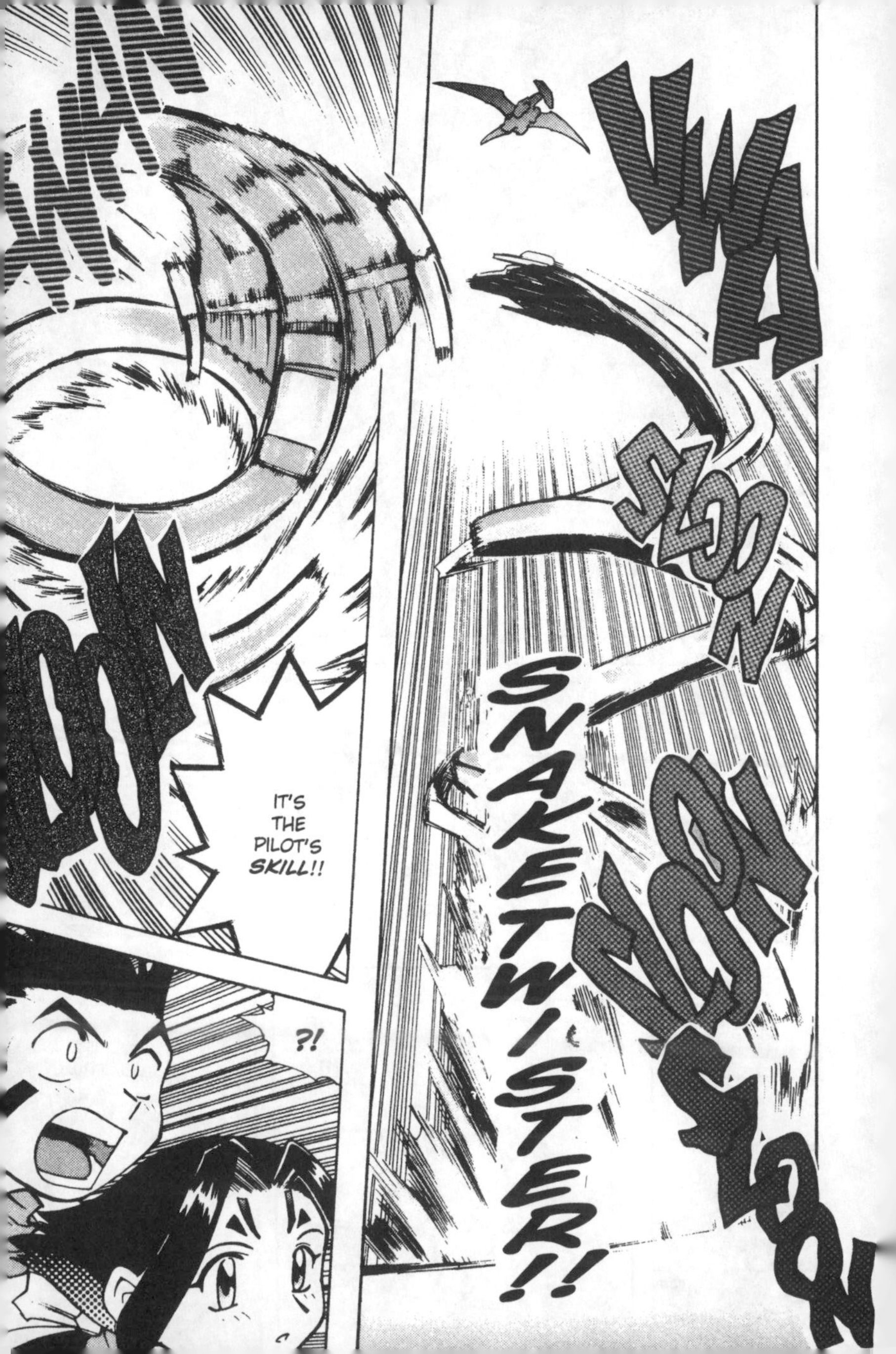
IT'S THE PILOT'S SKILL!!
?!
SNAKE TWISTER!!

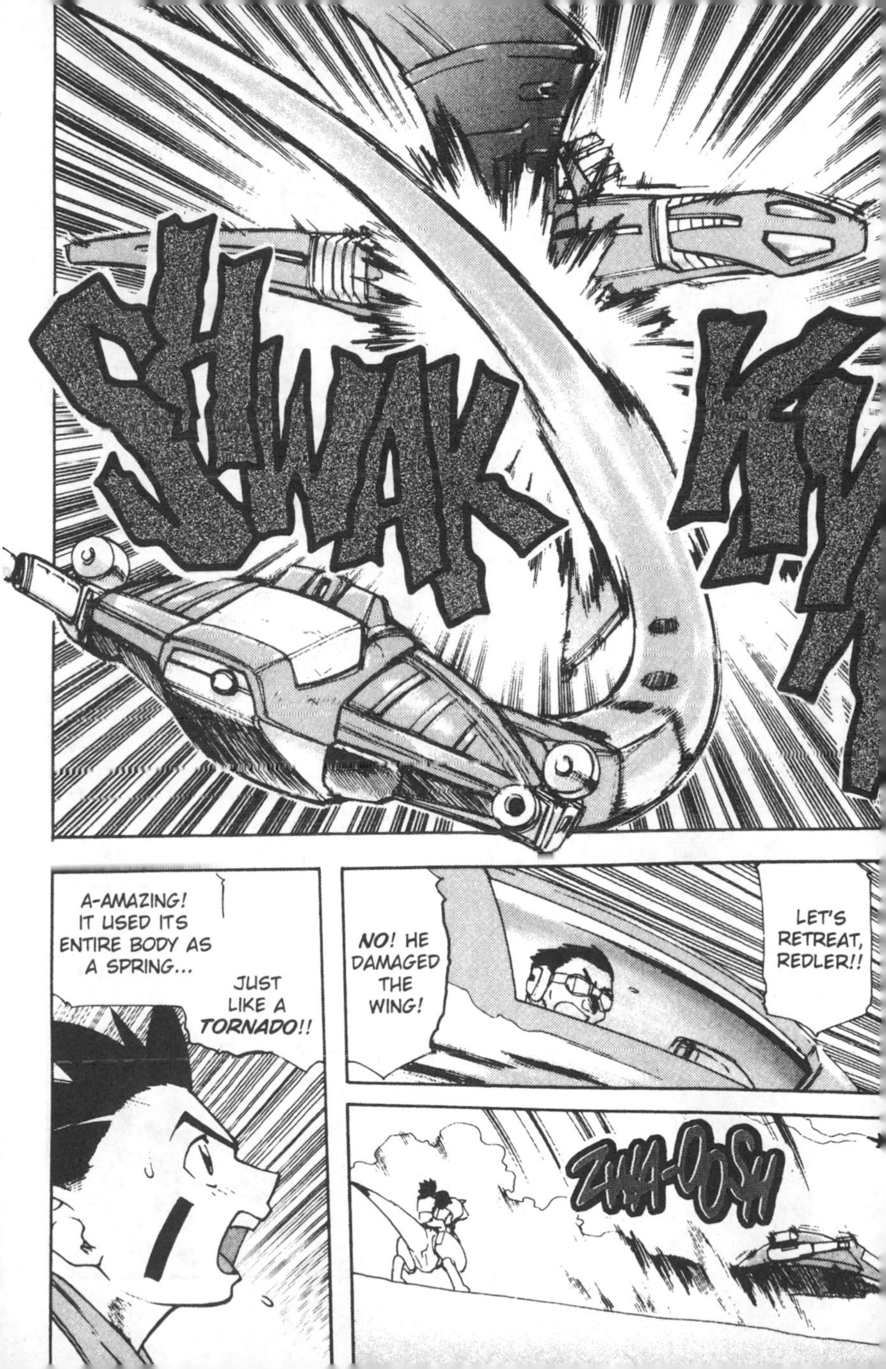
SHWAK
A-AMAZING! IT USED ITS ENTIRE BODY AS A SPRING...
JUST LIKE A *TORNADO*!!
NO! HE DAMAGED THE WING!
LET'S RETREAT, REDLER!!
ZWA-OOSH

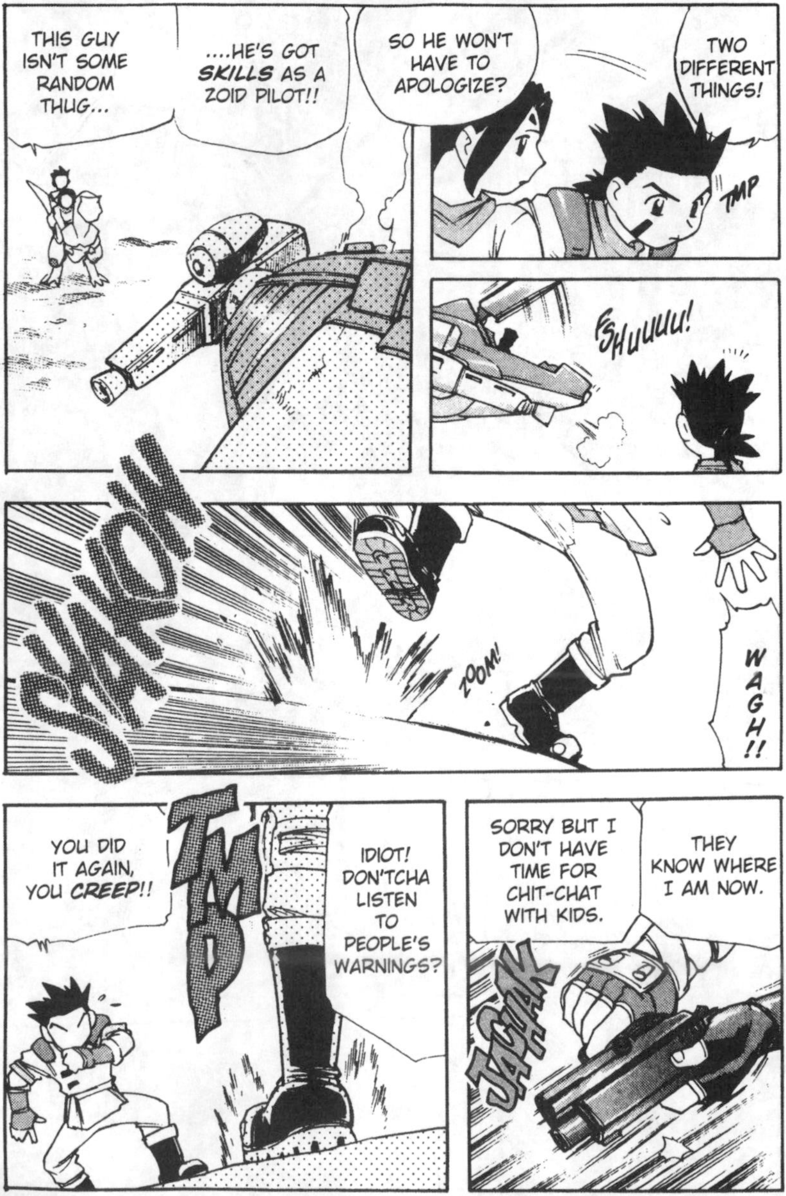
THIS GUY ISN'T SOME RANDOM THUG...
....HE'S GOT SKILLS AS A ZOID PILOT!!
SO HE WON'T HAVE TO APOLOGIZE?
TWO DIFFERENT THINGS!
TMP
FSHUUUU!
SHAKOW
ZOOM!
WAGH!!
YOU DID IT AGAIN, YOU CREEP!!
TMP
IDIOT! DON'TCHA LISTEN TO PEOPLE'S WARNINGS?
SORRY BUT I DON'T HAVE TIME FOR CHIT-CHAT WITH KIDS.
THEY KNOW WHERE I AM NOW.
JACHAK

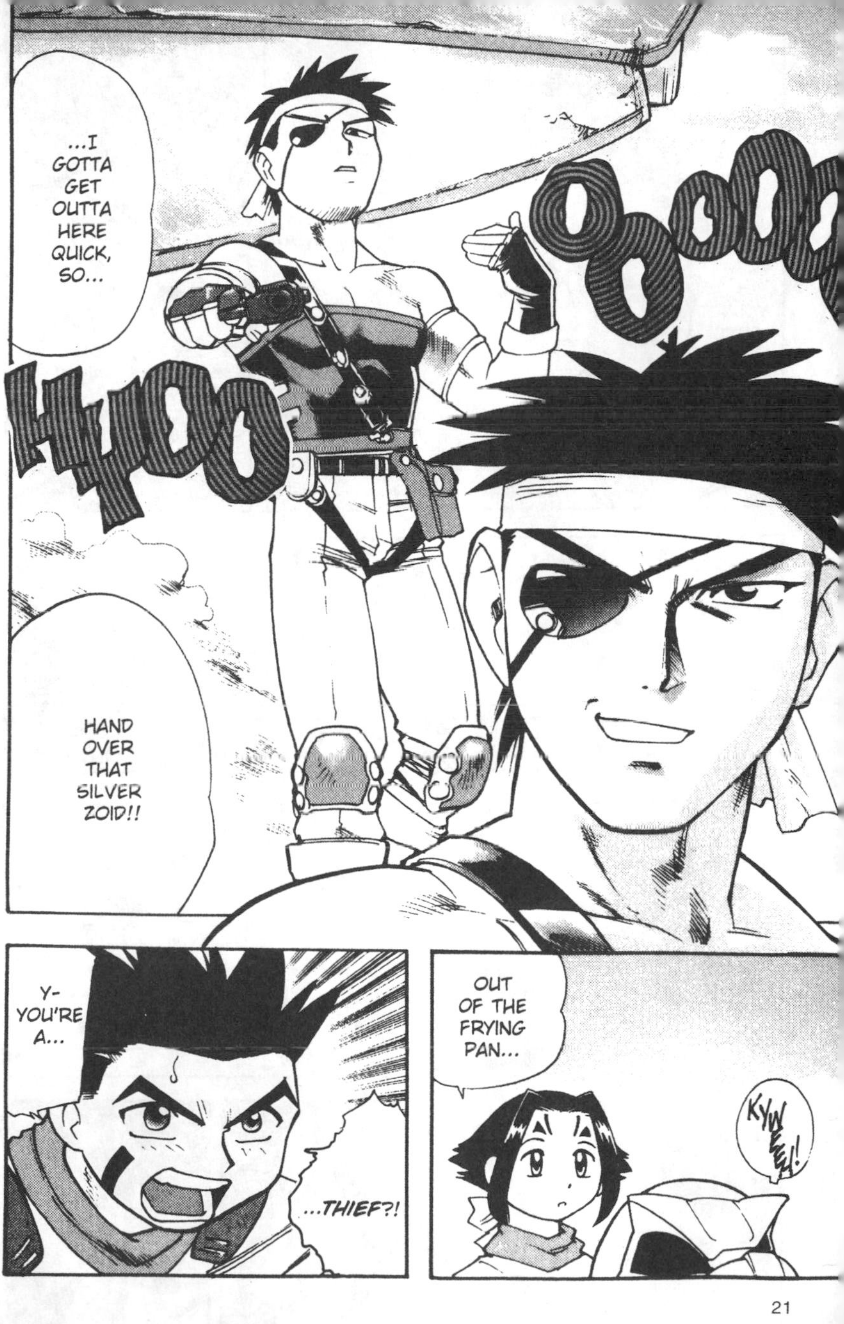
...I GOTTA GET OUTTA HERE QUICK, SO...
HAND OVER THAT SILVER ZOID!!
Y- YOU'RE A...
...THIEF?!
OUT OF THE FRYING PAN...

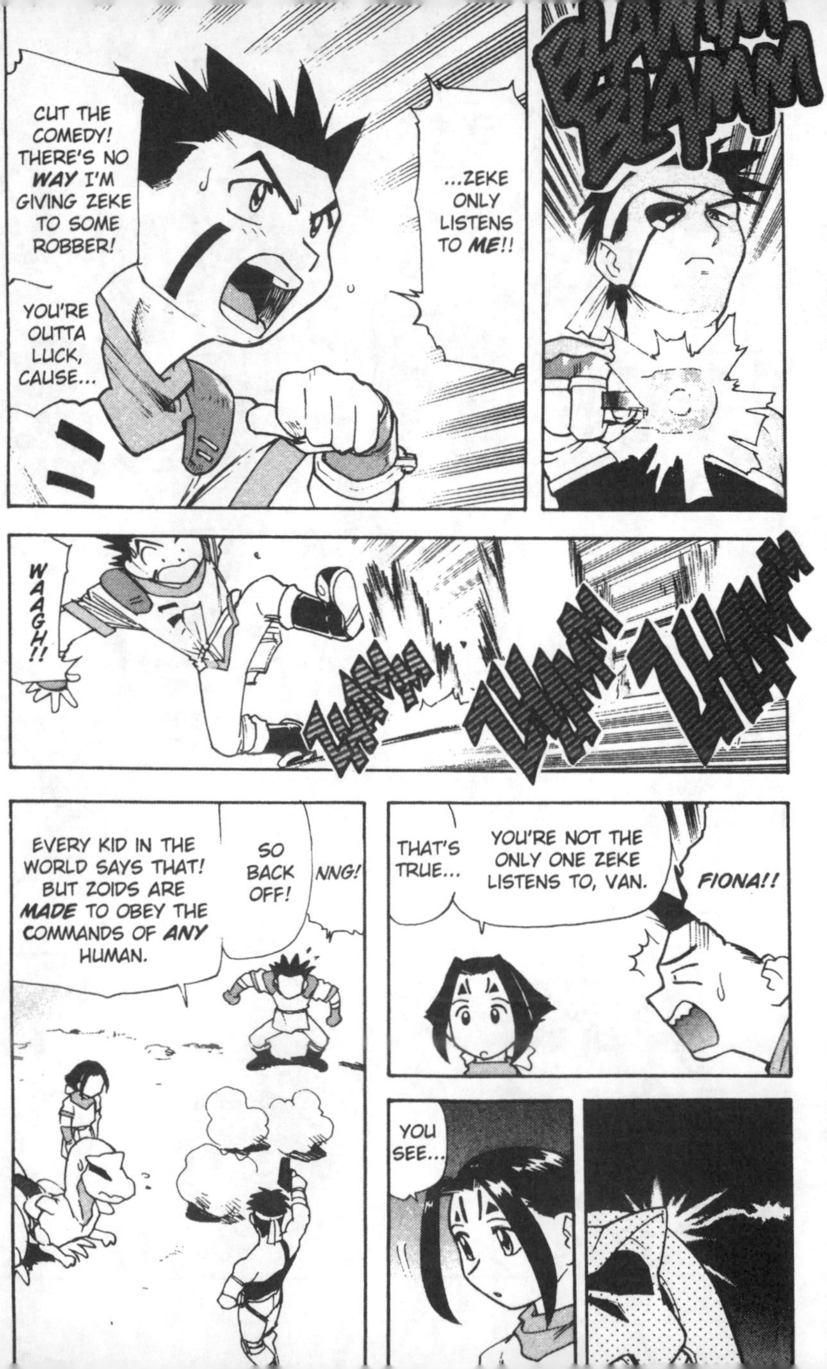
CUT THE COMEDY! THERE'S NO **WAY** I'M GIVING ZEKE TO SOME ROBBER!
YOU'RE OUTTA LUCK, CAUSE...
...ZEKE ONLY LISTENS TO **ME**!!
WAAAGH!!
EVERY KID IN THE WORLD SAYS THAT! BUT ZOIDS ARE **MADE** TO OBEY THE COMMANDS OF **ANY** HUMAN.
SO BACK OFF!
NNG!
THAT'S TRUE...
YOU'RE NOT THE ONLY ONE ZEKE LISTENS TO, VAN.
FIONA!!
YOU SEE...

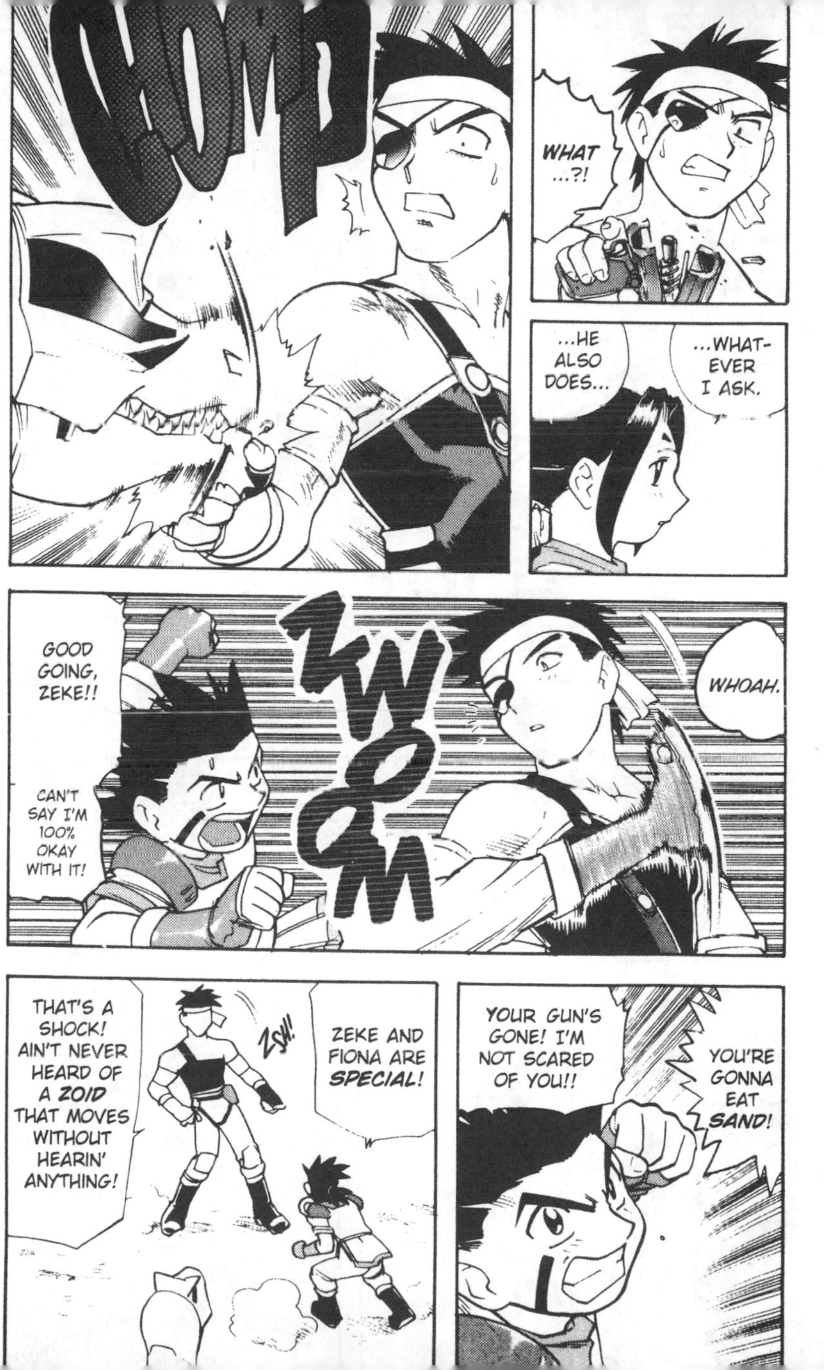
CHOMP
WHAT ...?!
...HE ALSO DOES...
...WHAT-EVER I ASK.
GOOD GOING, ZEKE!!
CAN'T SAY I'M 100% OKAY WITH IT!
ZWOOM
WHOAH.
THAT'S A SHOCK! AIN'T NEVER HEARD OF A ZOID THAT MOVES WITHOUT HEARIN' ANYTHING!
ZSH!
ZEKE AND FIONA ARE SPECIAL!
YOUR GUN'S GONE! I'M NOT SCARED OF YOU!!
YOU'RE GONNA EAT SAND!

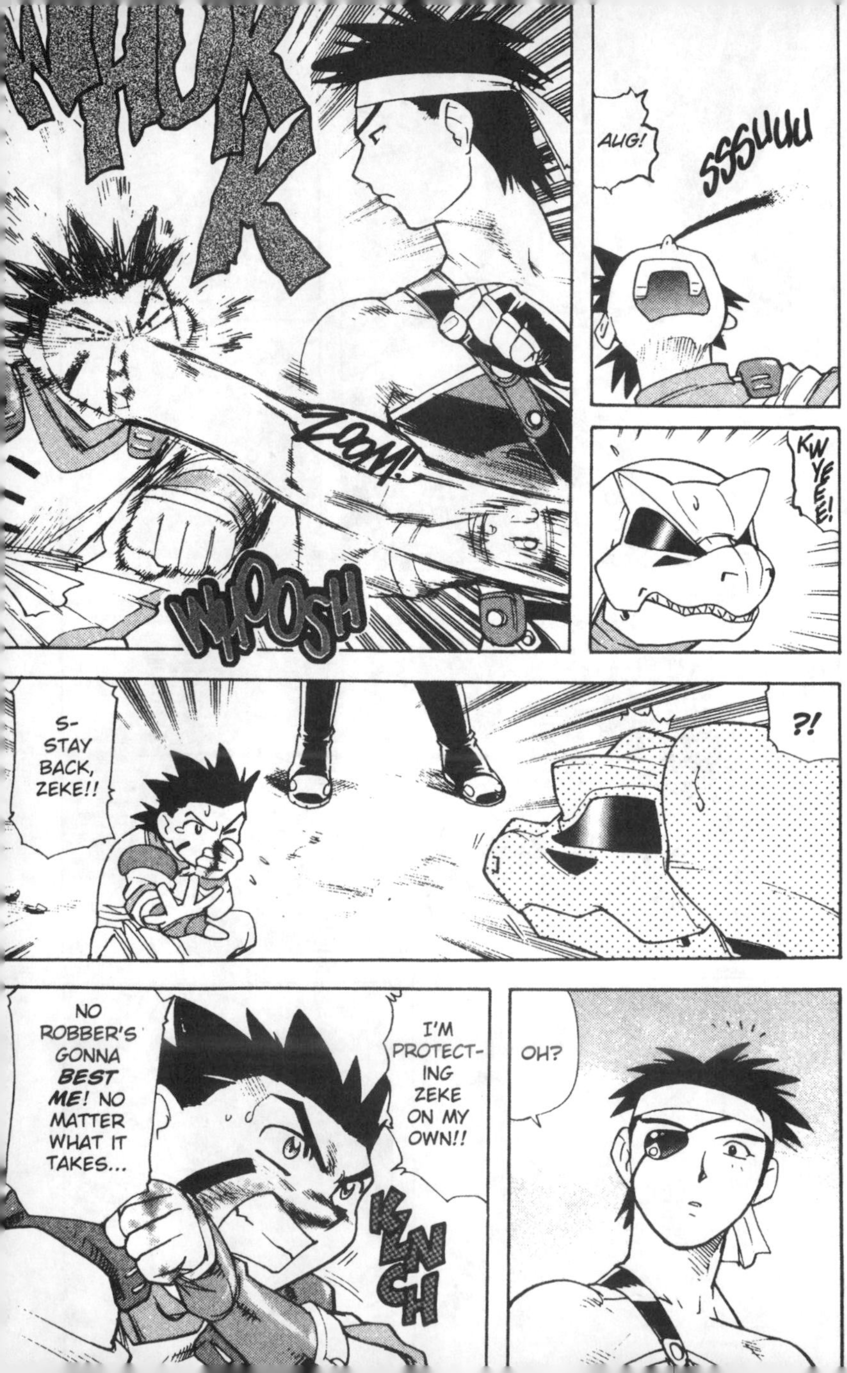
WHUKK
ZOOM!
WHOOSH
AUG!
SSSUUU
KWYEEE!
S-STAY BACK, ZEKE!!
?!
NO ROBBER'S GONNA ***BEST ME!*** NO MATTER WHAT IT TAKES...
I'M PROTECT-ING ZEKE ON MY OWN!!
KLNCH
OH?

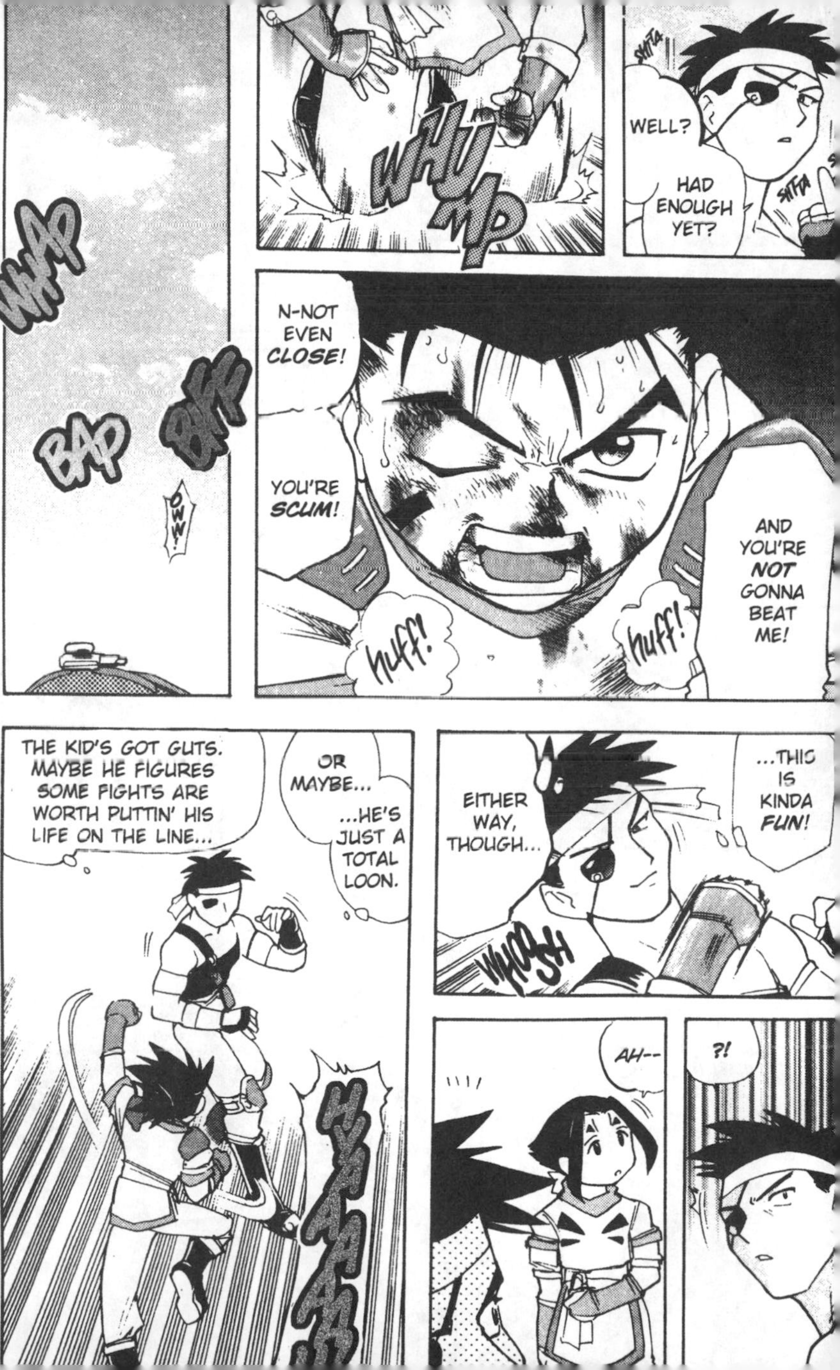
WHAP
BAP
OWW!
WHUMP
WELL?
HAD ENOUGH YET?
N-NOT EVEN CLOSE!
YOU'RE SCUM!
huff!
huff!
AND YOU'RE NOT GONNA BEAT ME!
THE KID'S GOT GUTS. MAYBE HE FIGURES SOME FIGHTS ARE WORTH PUTTIN' HIS LIFE ON THE LINE...
OR MAYBE...
...HE'S JUST A TOTAL LOON.
EITHER WAY, THOUGH...
...THIS IS KINDA FUN!
WHOOSH
AH--
?!

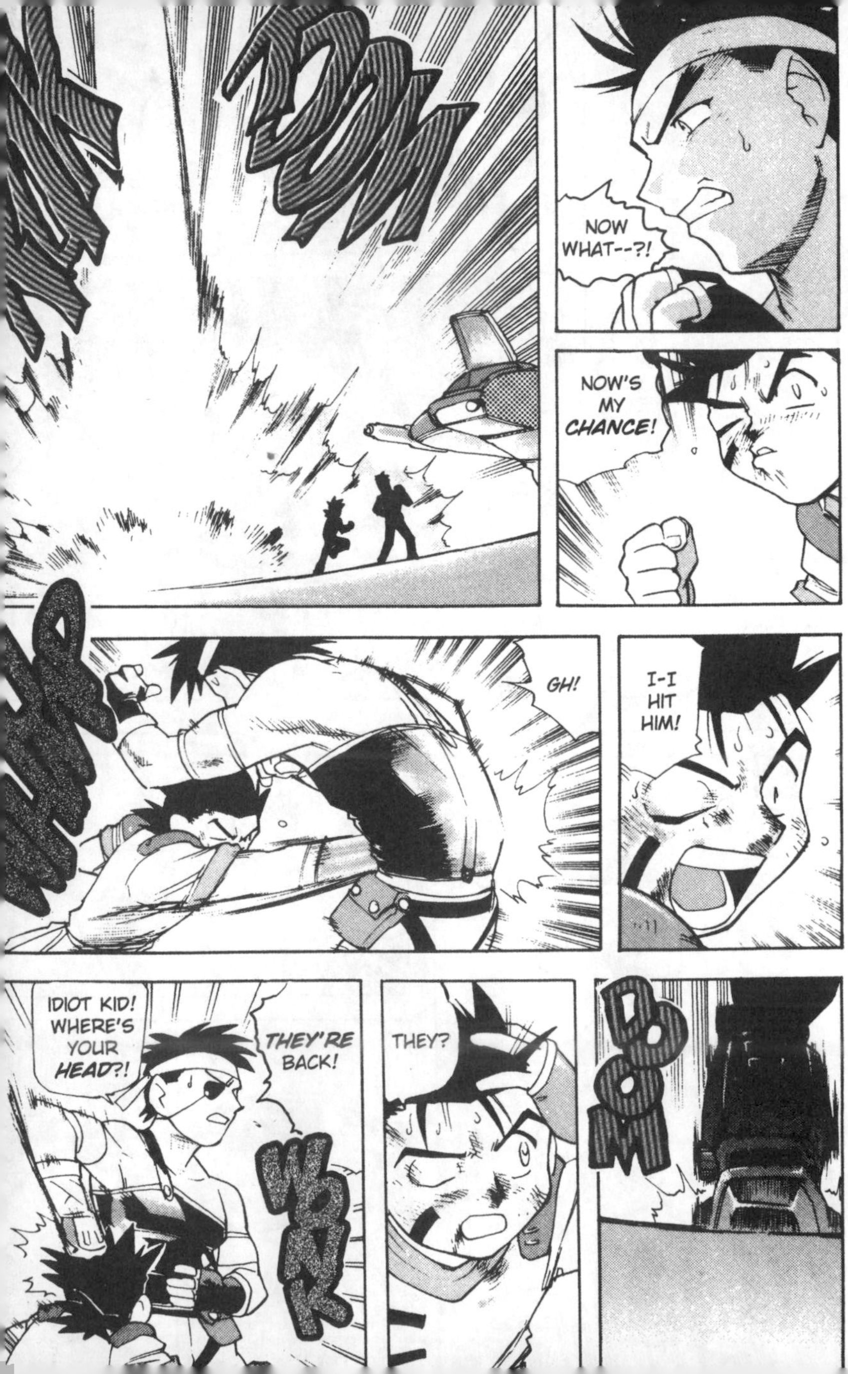
NOW WHAT--?!
NOW'S MY *CHANCE!*
GH!
I-I HIT HIM!
IDIOT KID! WHERE'S YOUR *HEAD?!*
THEY'RE BACK!
THEY?
DOOM

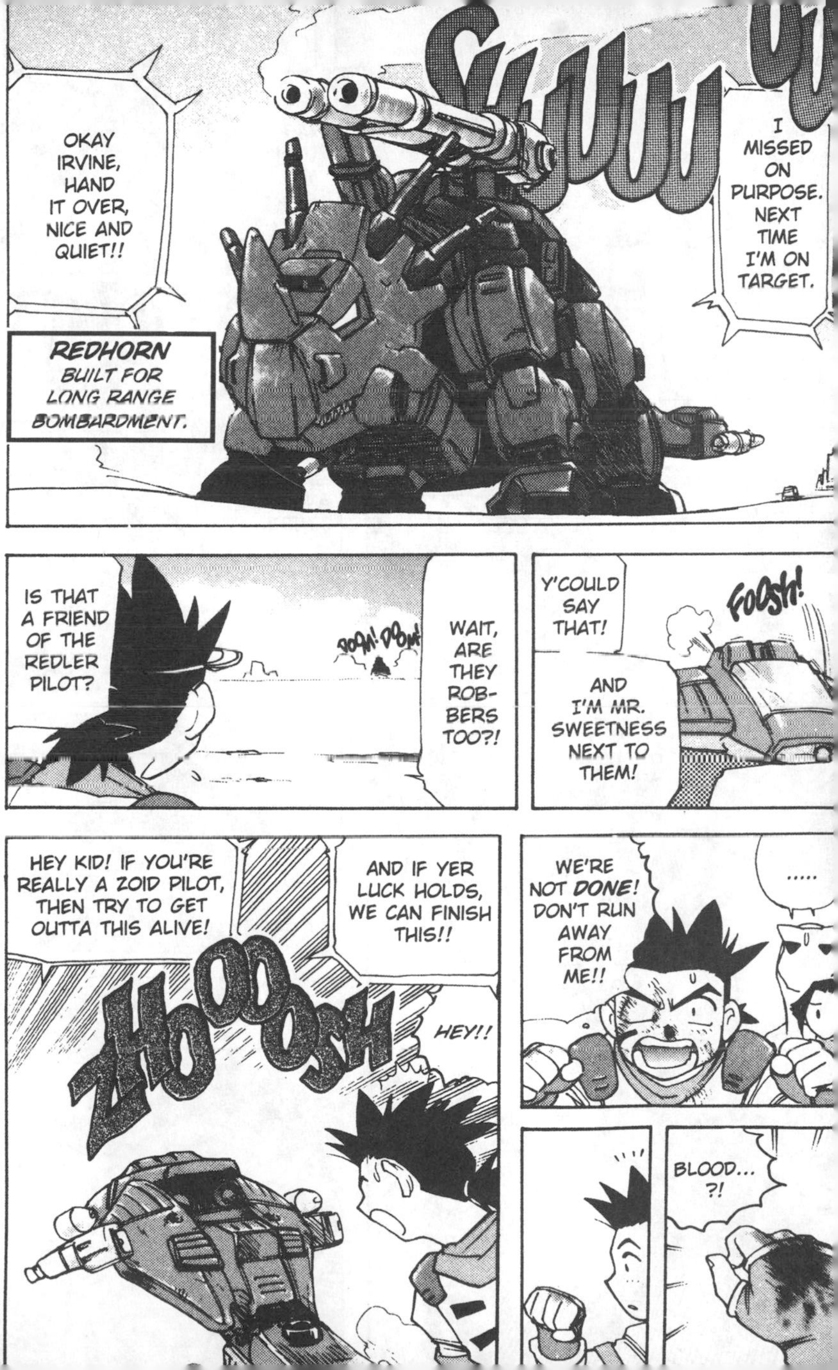
SHUUUU
OKAY IRVINE, HAND IT OVER, NICE AND QUIET!!
REDHORN BUILT FOR LONG RANGE BOMBARDMENT.
I MISSED ON PURPOSE. NEXT TIME I'M ON TARGET.
IS THAT A FRIEND OF THE REDLER PILOT?
WAIT, ARE THEY ROB-BERS TOO?!
Y'COULD SAY THAT!
FOOSH!
AND I'M MR. SWEETNESS NEXT TO THEM!
HEY KID! IF YOU'RE REALLY A ZOID PILOT, THEN TRY TO GET OUTTA THIS ALIVE!
AND IF YER LUCK HOLDS, WE CAN FINISH THIS!!
ZHOOOOSH
HEY!!
WE'RE NOT DONE! DON'T RUN AWAY FROM ME!!
.....
BLOOD... ?!

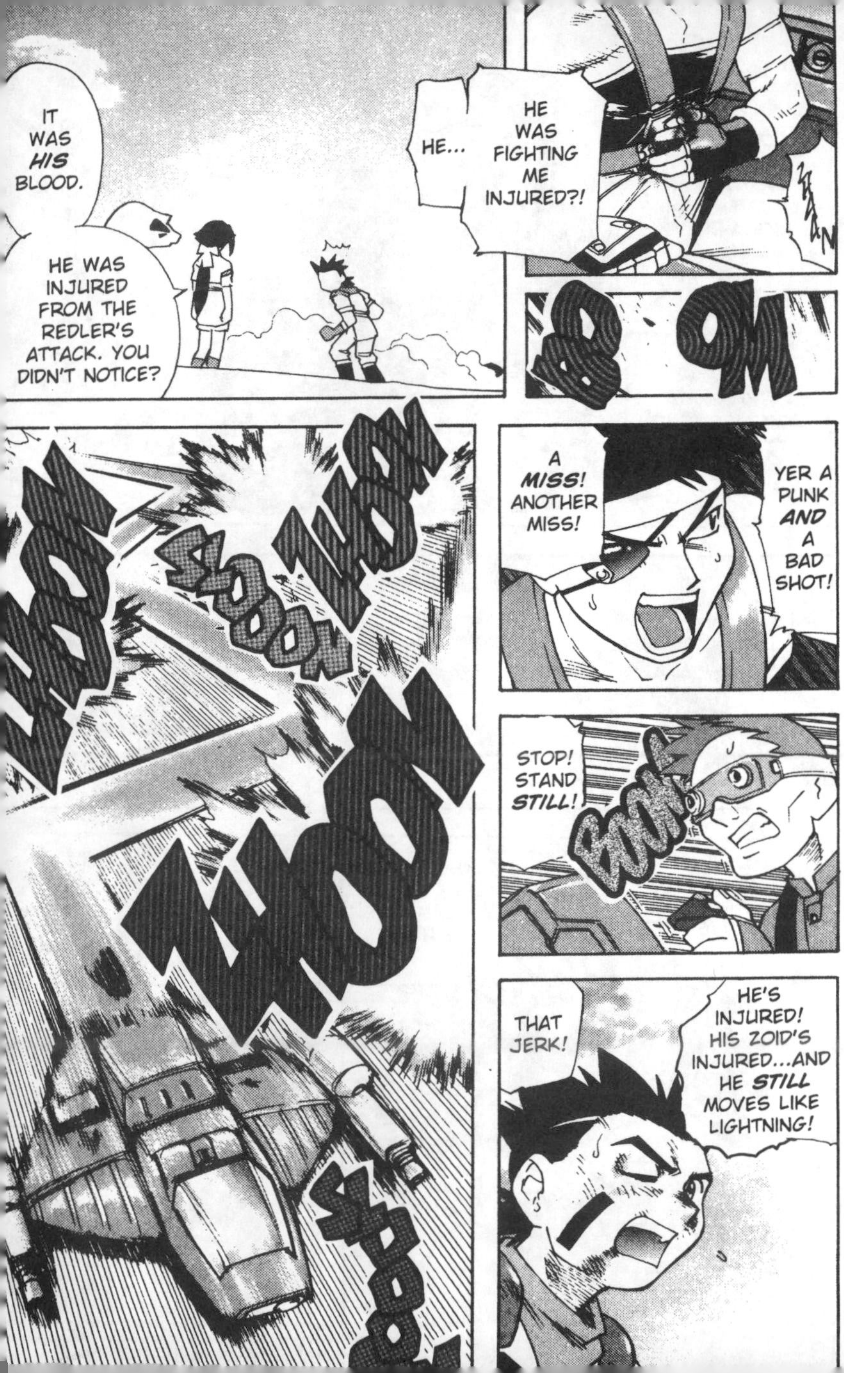
IT WAS HIS BLOOD.
HE WAS INJURED FROM THE REDLER'S ATTACK. YOU DIDN'T NOTICE?
HE...
HE WAS FIGHTING ME INJURED?!
A MISS! ANOTHER MISS!
YER A PUNK AND A BAD SHOT!
STOP! STAND STILL!
BOOM
THAT JERK!
HE'S INJURED! HIS ZOID'S INJURED...AND HE STILL MOVES LIKE LIGHTNING!

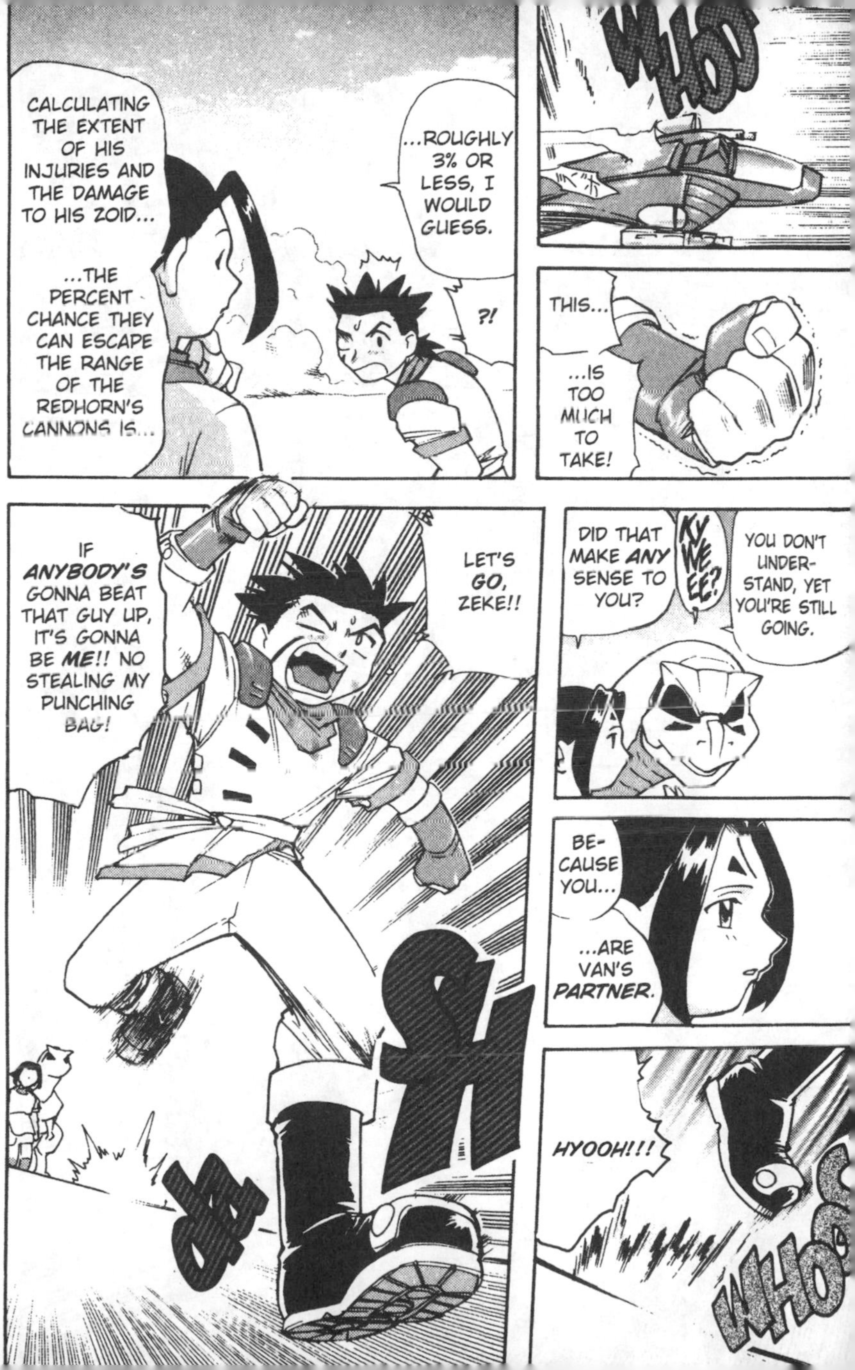

CALCULATING THE EXTENT OF HIS INJURIES AND THE DAMAGE TO HIS ZOID...
...THE PERCENT CHANCE THEY CAN ESCAPE THE RANGE OF THE REDHORN'S CANNONS IS...
...ROUGHLY 3% OR LESS, I WOULD GUESS.
?!
THIS...
...IS TOO MUCH TO TAKE!
IF ANYBODY'S GONNA BEAT THAT GUY UP, IT'S GONNA BE ME!! NO STEALING MY PUNCHING BAG!
LET'S GO, ZEKE!!
DID THAT MAKE ANY SENSE TO YOU?
KYWEEE?
YOU DON'T UNDERSTAND, YET YOU'RE STILL GOING.
BECAUSE YOU...
...ARE VAN'S PARTNER.
HYOOH!!!

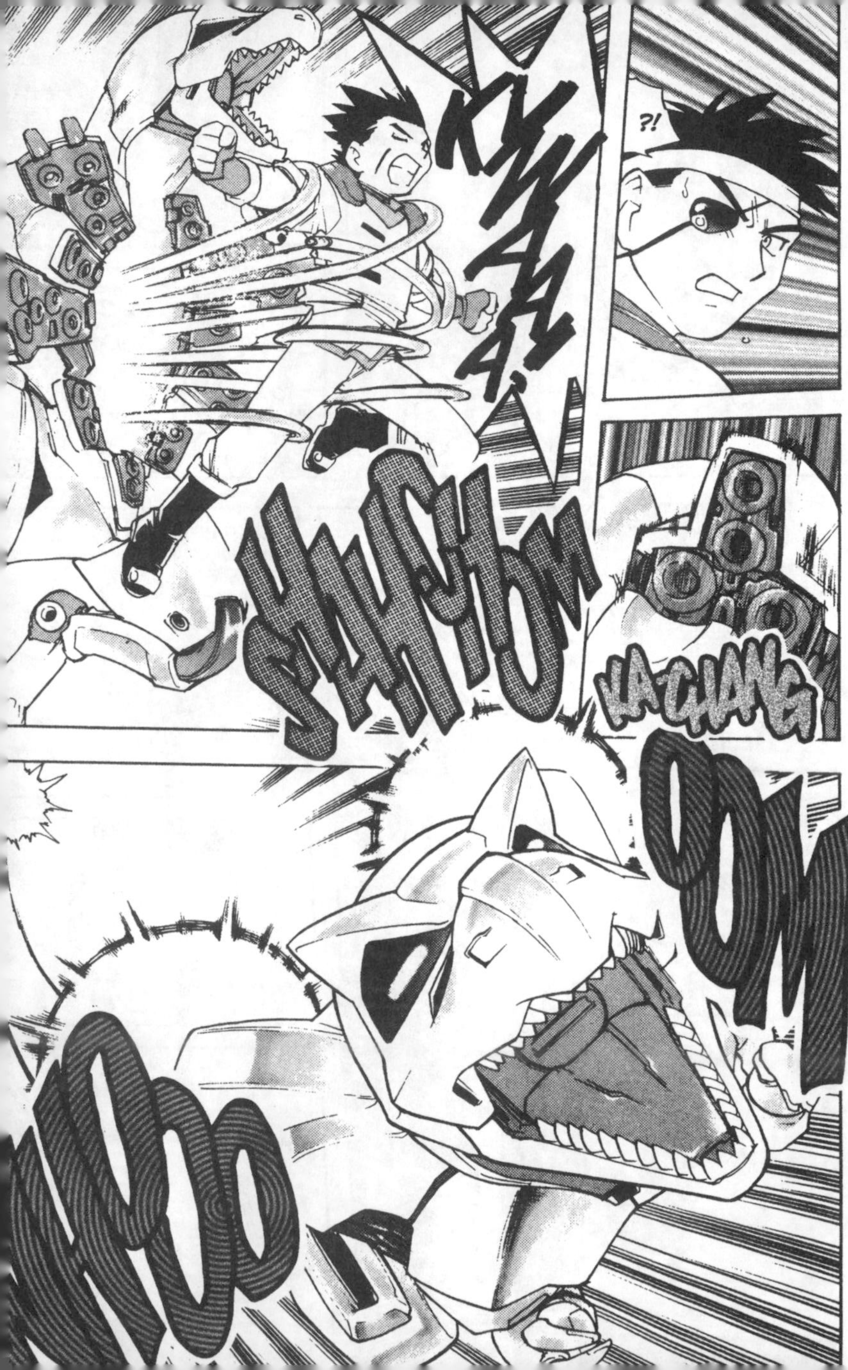
KWAAAA!
SHHSHOM
?!
KACHANG
WHOOOO
OOM

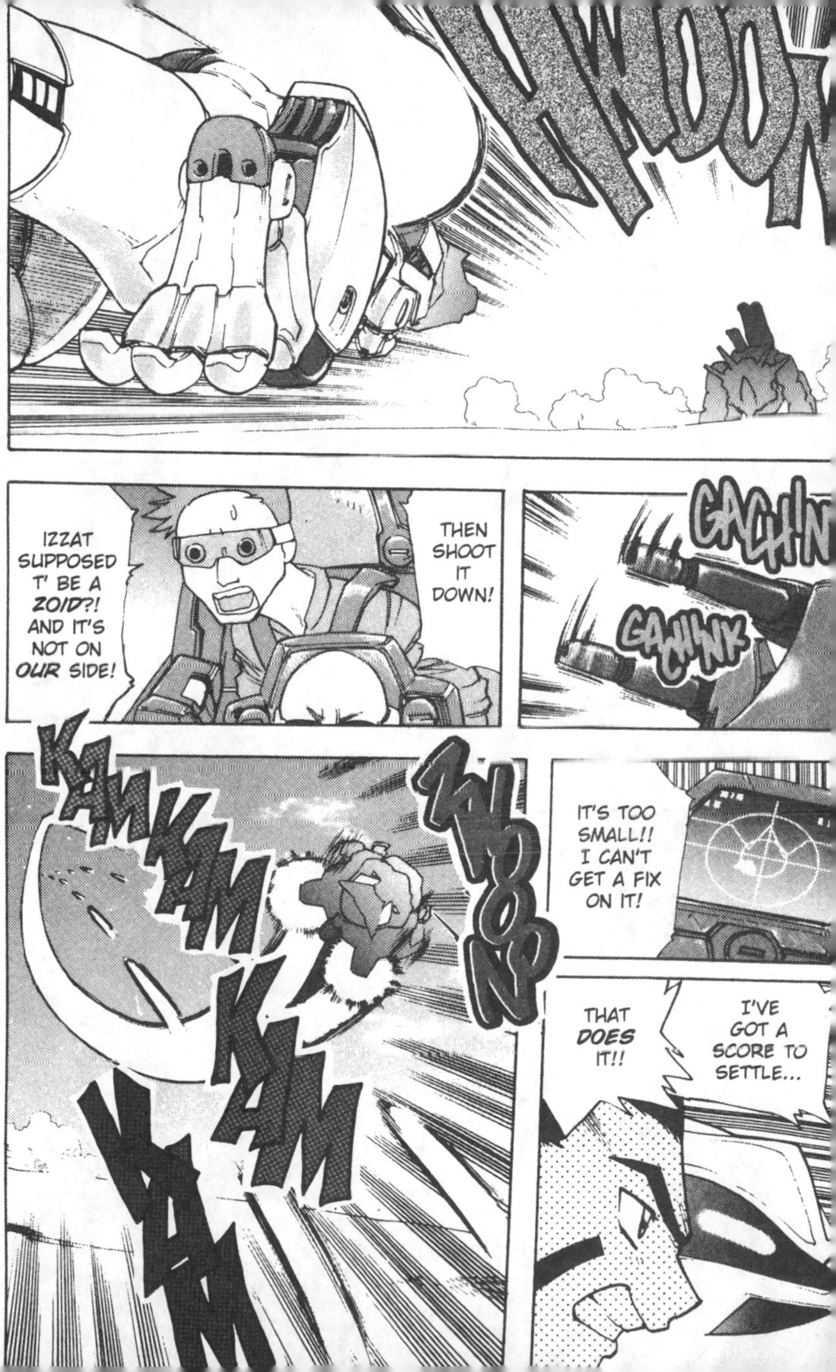
GACHINK
GACHINK
THEN SHOOT IT DOWN!
IZZAT SUPPOSED T' BE A *ZOID*?! AND IT'S NOT ON *OUR* SIDE!
IT'S TOO SMALL!! I CAN'T GET A FIX ON IT!
I'VE GOT A SCORE TO SETTLE...
THAT *DOES* IT!!
KAM KAM KAM
KAM KAM

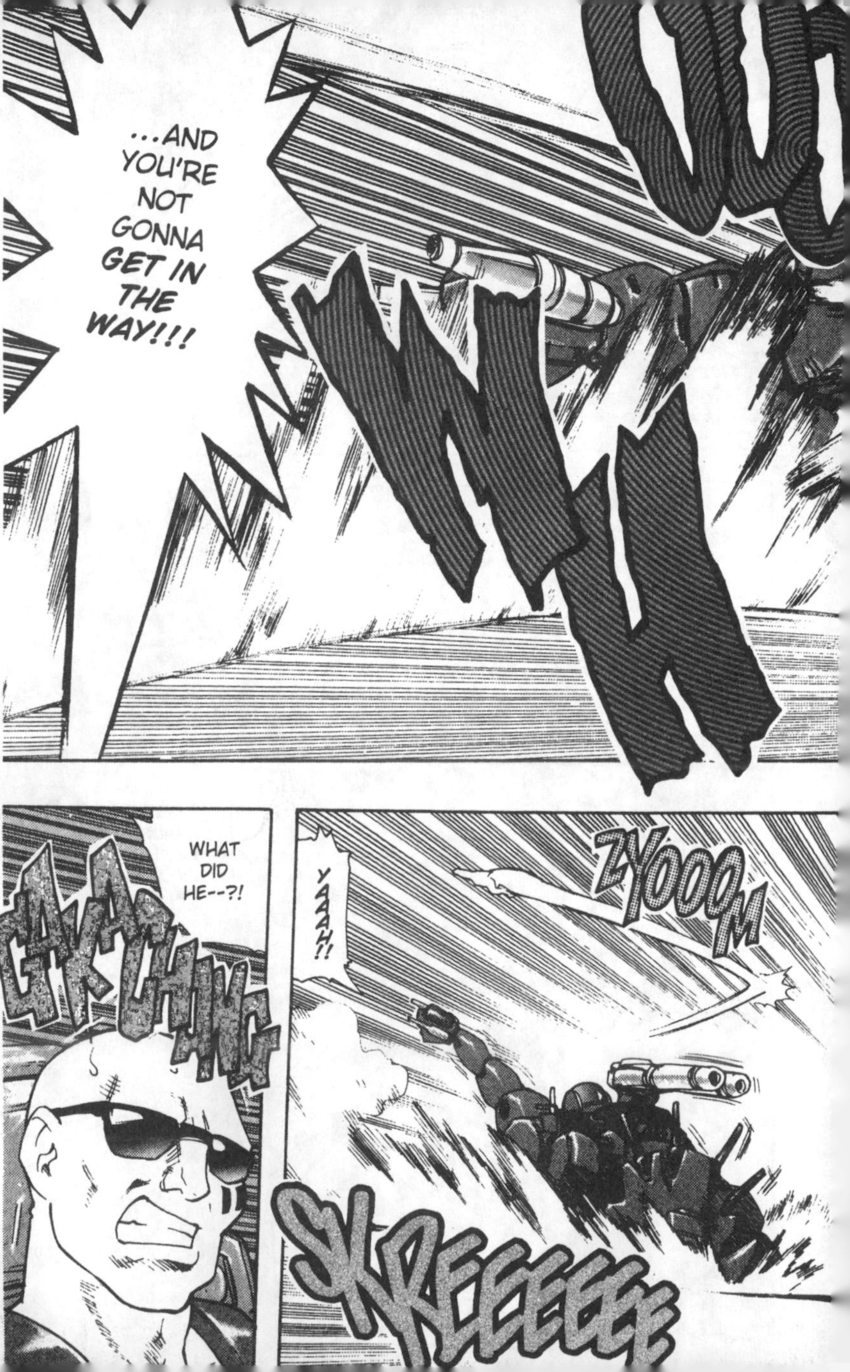
...AND YOU'RE NOT GONNA GET IN THE WAY!!!
YAAAH!!
ZYOOOM
SKREEEEEE
WHAT DID HE--?!
GACHING

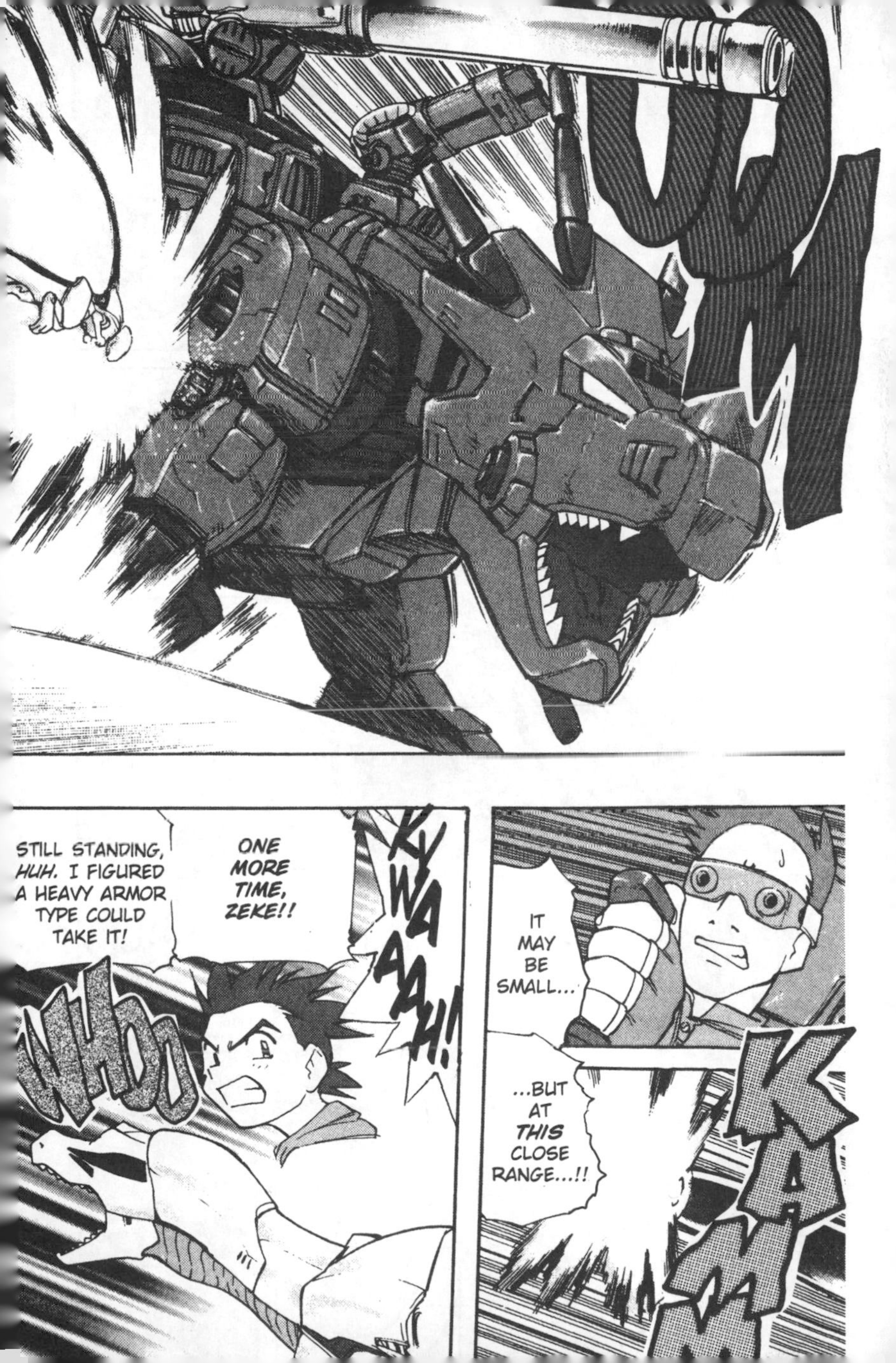
STILL STANDING, *HUH*. I FIGURED A HEAVY ARMOR TYPE COULD TAKE IT!
ONE MORE TIME, ZEKE!!
IT MAY BE SMALL...
...BUT AT *THIS* CLOSE RANGE...!!

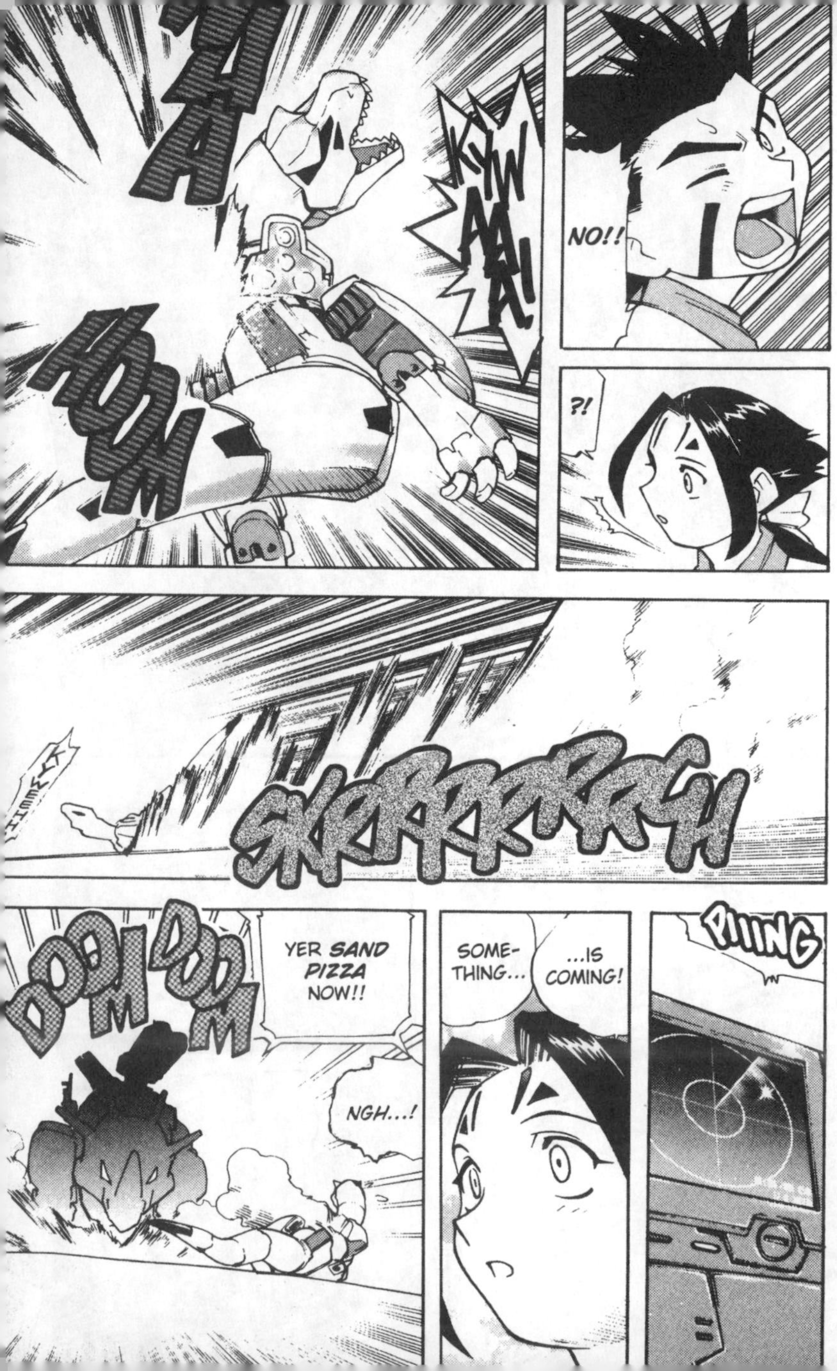
NO!!
?!
DOOM DOOM
YER SAND PIZZA NOW!!
NGH...!
SOME-THING...
...IS COMING!
PIIING

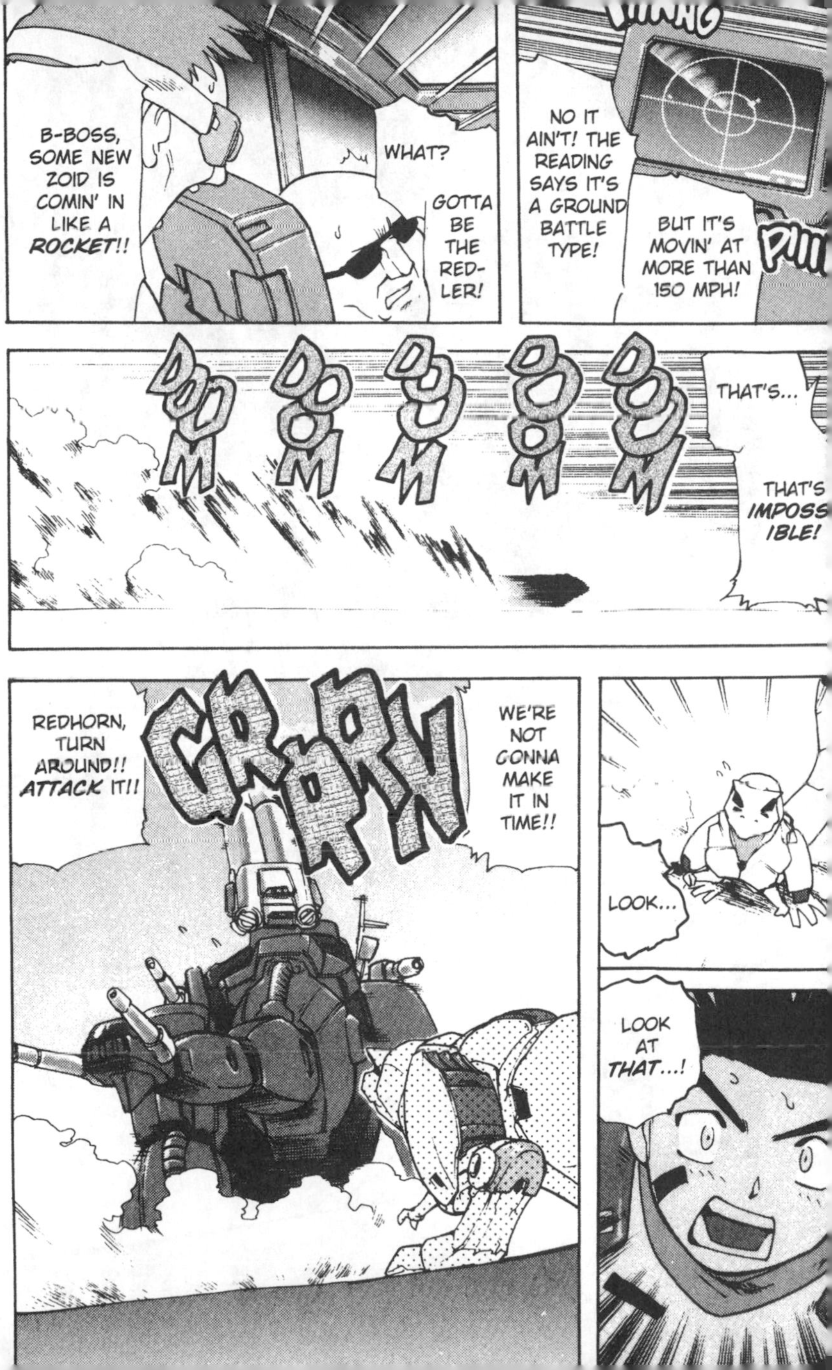
B-BOSS, SOME NEW ZOID IS COMIN' IN LIKE A *ROCKET*!!
WHAT?
GOTTA BE THE RED-LER!
NO IT AIN'T! THE READING SAYS IT'S A GROUND BATTLE TYPE!
BUT IT'S MOVIN' AT MORE THAN 150 MPH!
DOOOM
DOOOM
DOOOM
DOOOM
DOOOM
THAT'S...
THAT'S *IMPOSSIBLE!*
REDHORN, TURN AROUND!! *ATTACK* IT!!
WE'RE NOT GONNA MAKE IT IN TIME!!
LOOK...
LOOK AT *THAT*...!

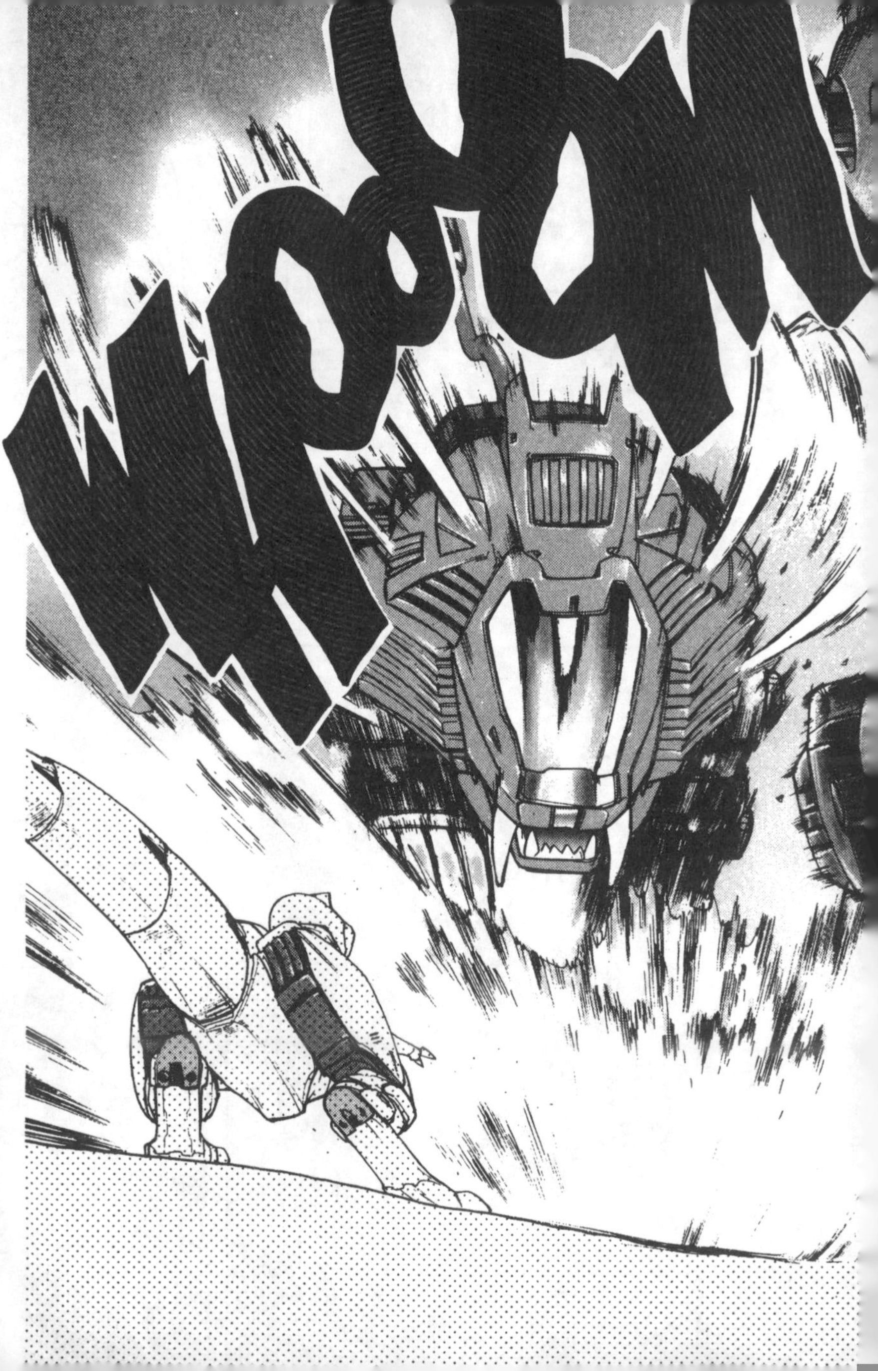

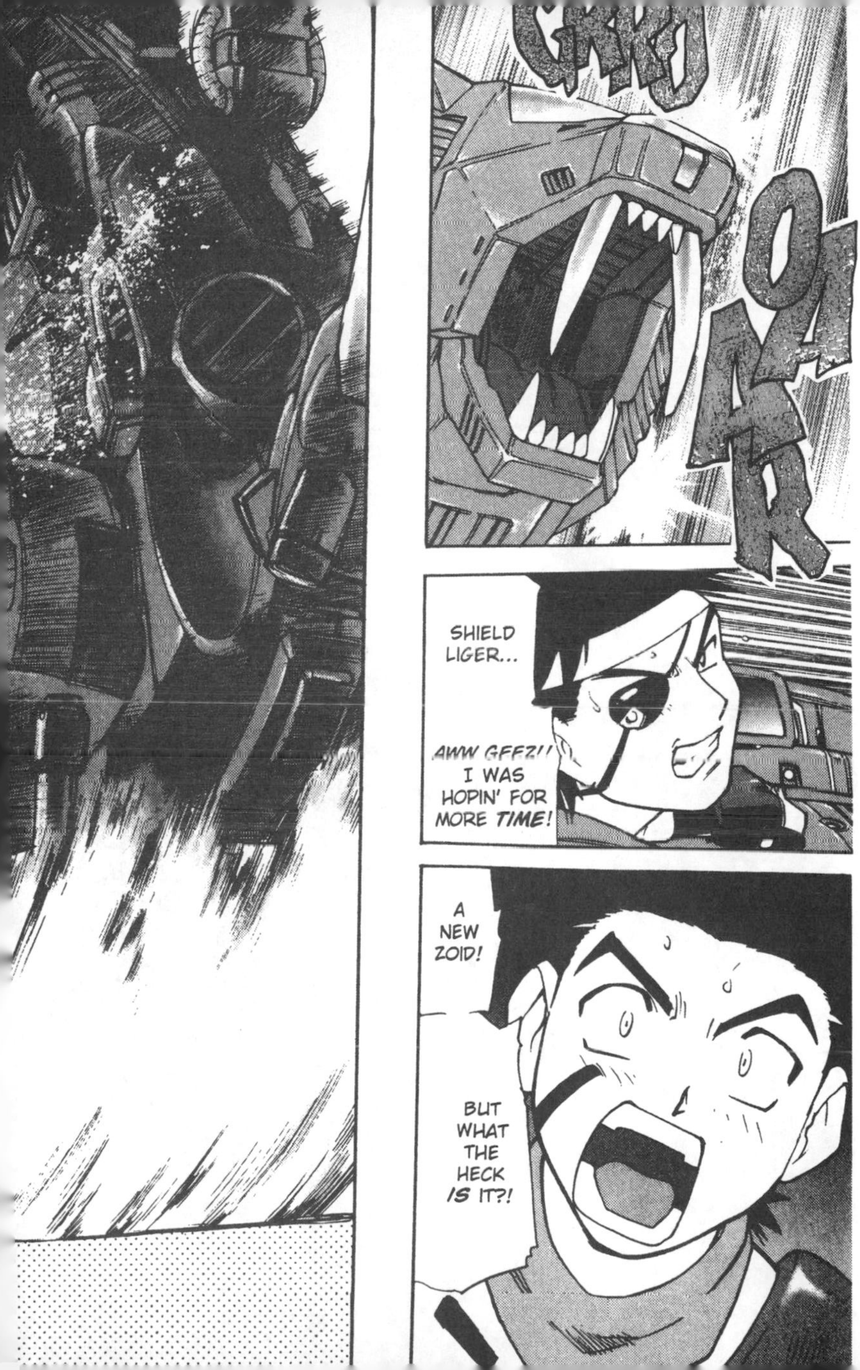
SHIELD LIGER...
AWW GEEZ!! I WAS HOPIN' FOR MORE TIME!
A NEW ZOID!
BUT WHAT THE HECK IS IT?!

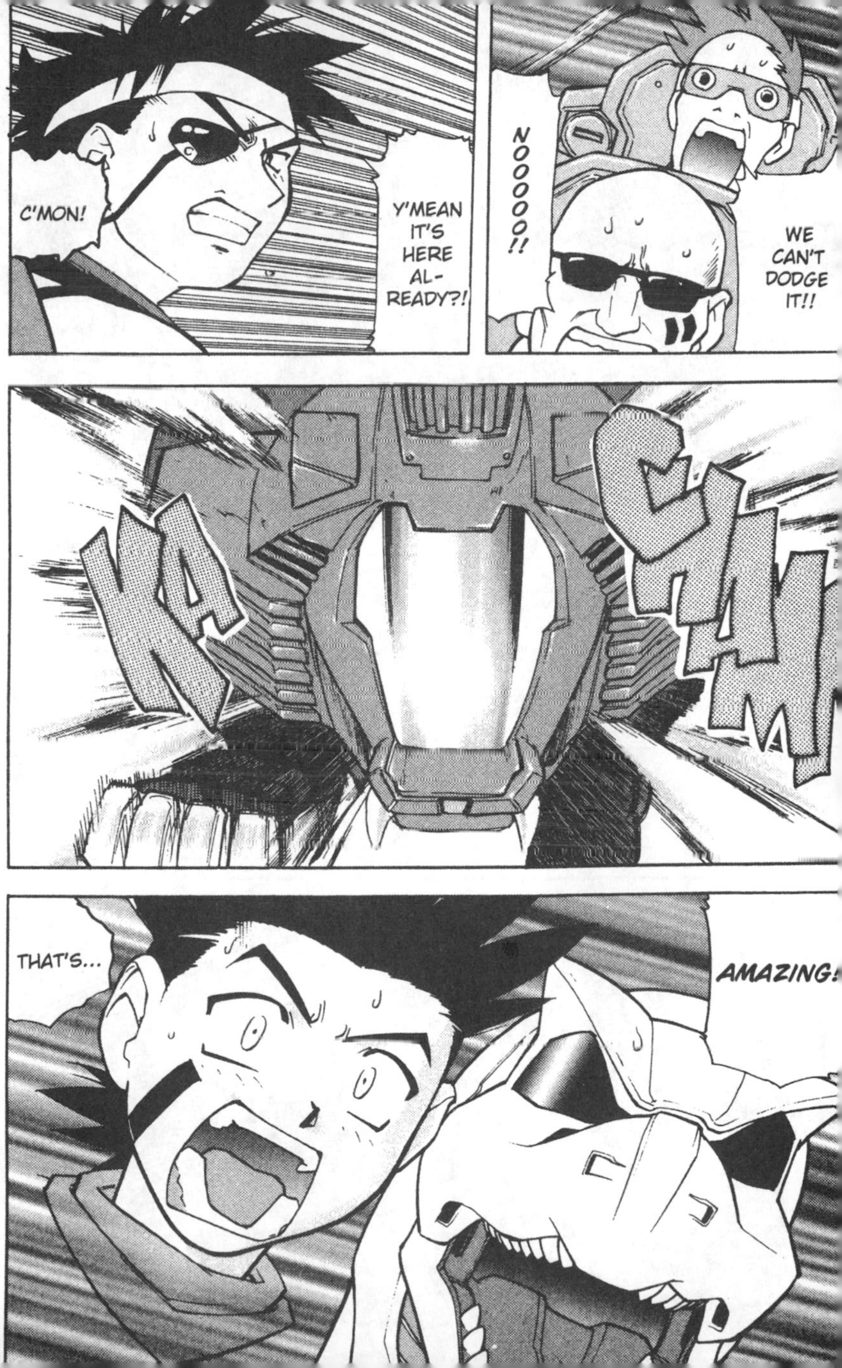
C'MON!
Y'MEAN IT'S HERE AL-READY?!
NOOOOOO!!
WE CAN'T DODGE IT!!
WA
CHAM
THAT'S...
AMAZING!

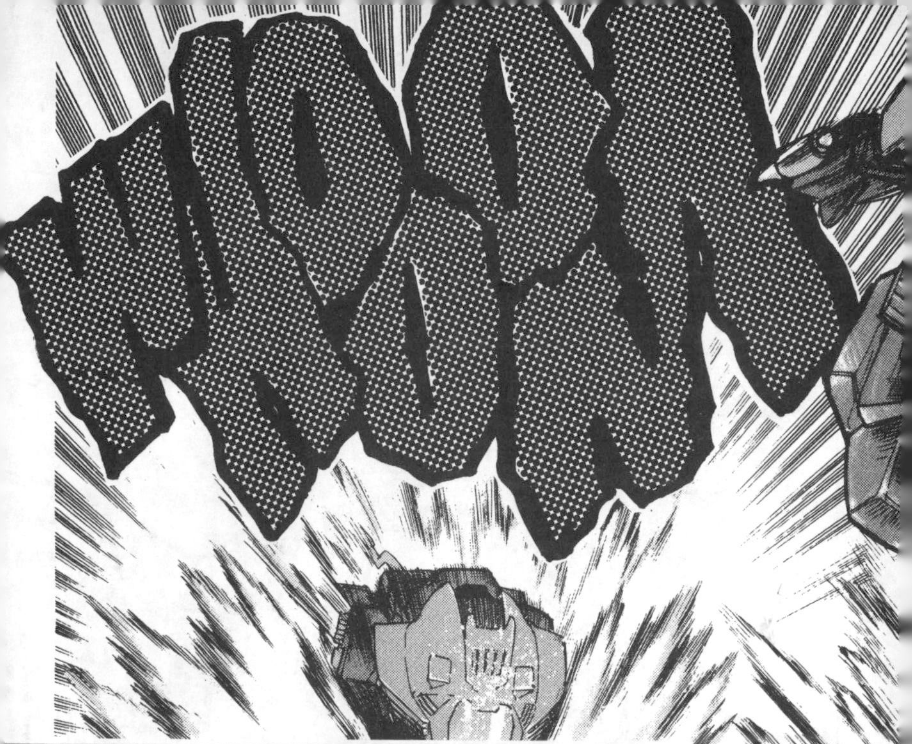

The Family Treasure

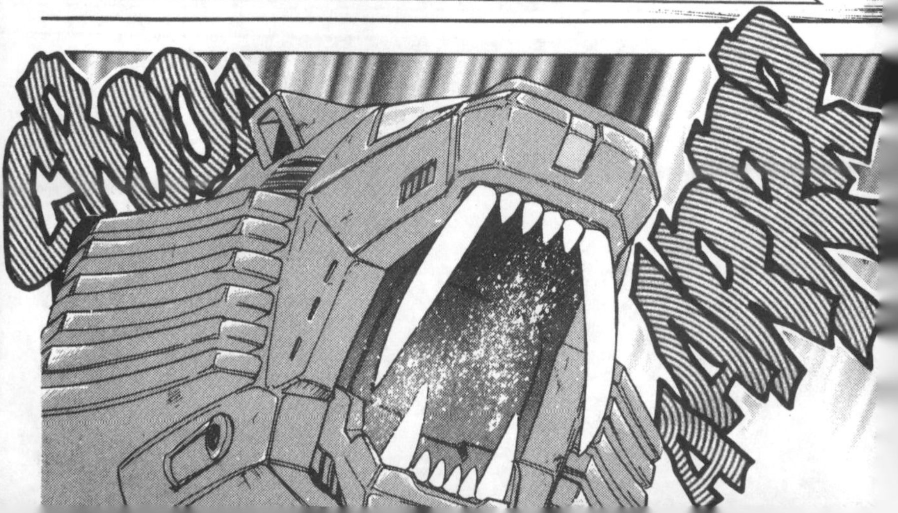

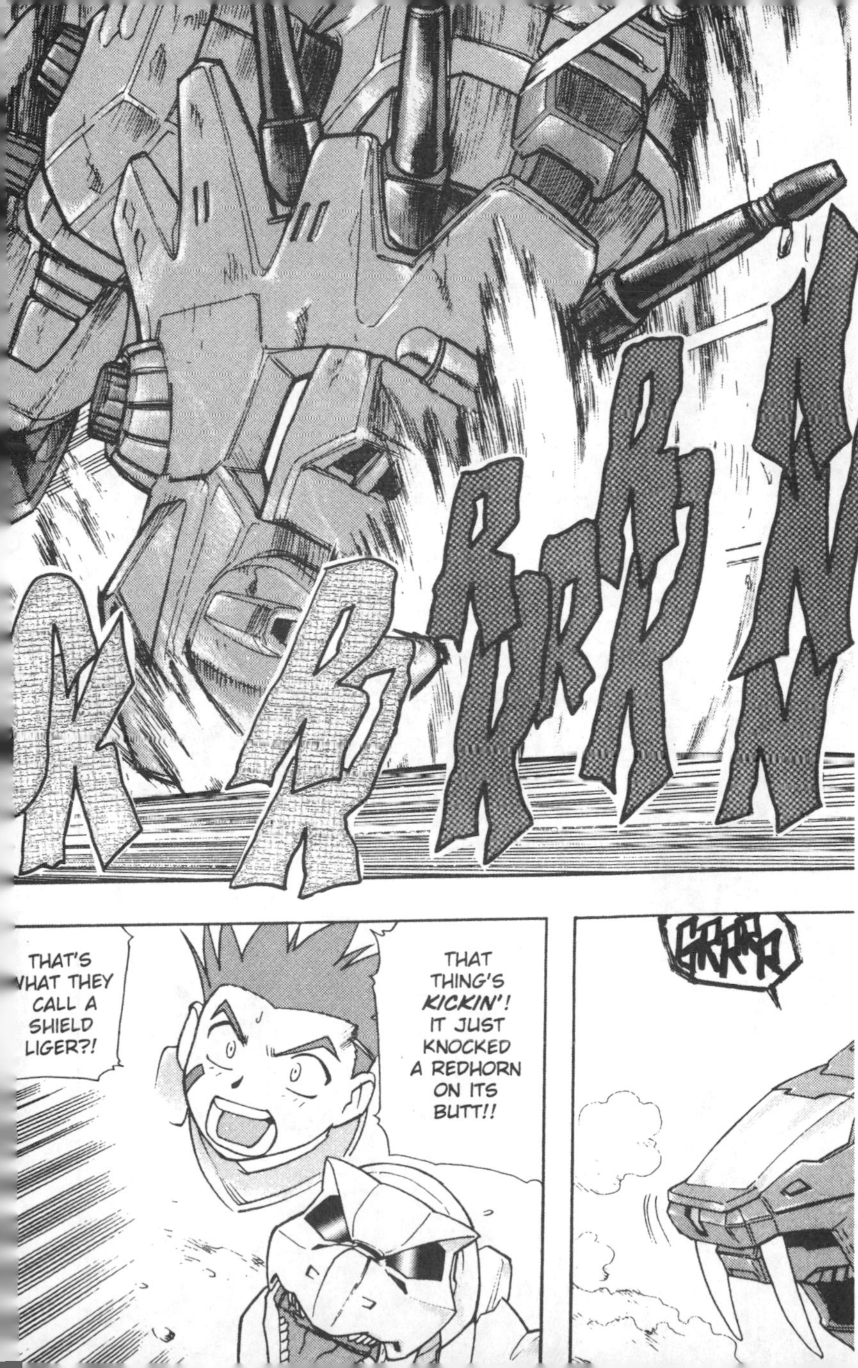
THAT'S WHAT THEY CALL A SHIELD LIGER?!
THAT THING'S *KICKIN'*! IT JUST KNOCKED A REDHORN ON ITS BUTT!!

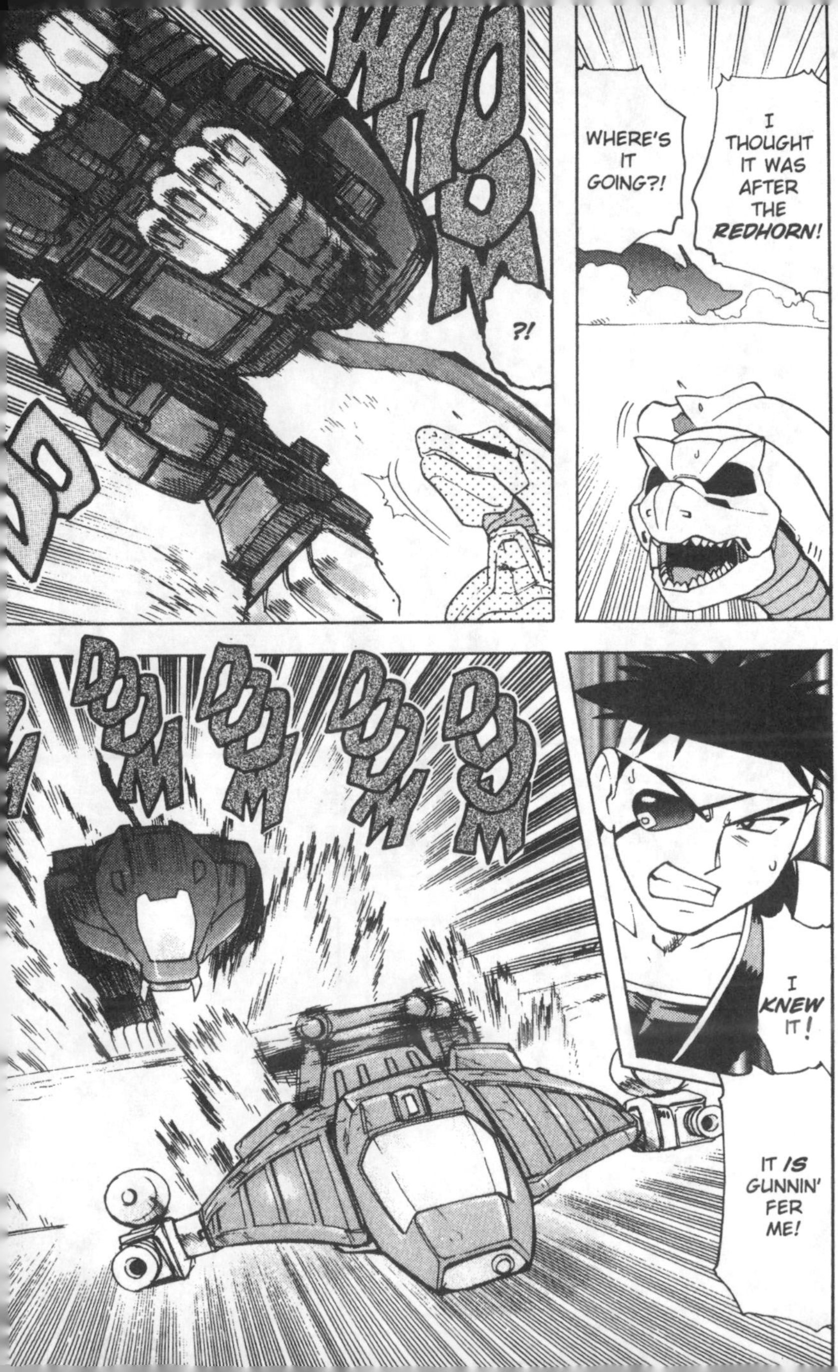
I THOUGHT IT WAS AFTER THE *REDHORN!*
WHERE'S IT GOING?!
WHOOM
?!
I *KNEW* IT!
IT *IS* GUNNIN' FER ME!
DOOM
DOOM
DOOM
DOOM

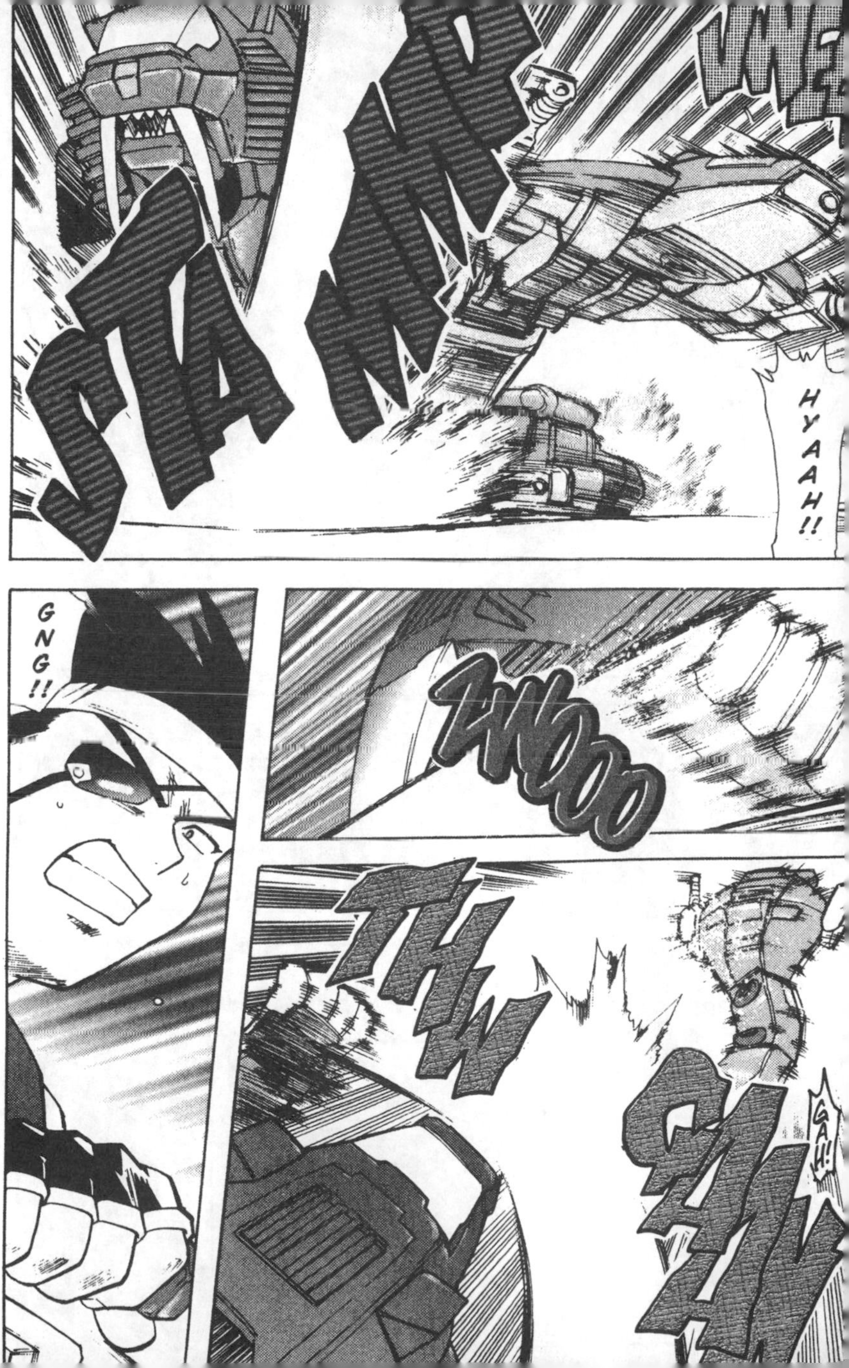
STAMP
HYAAAH!!
GNG!!
ZWOOO
THW
GAH!

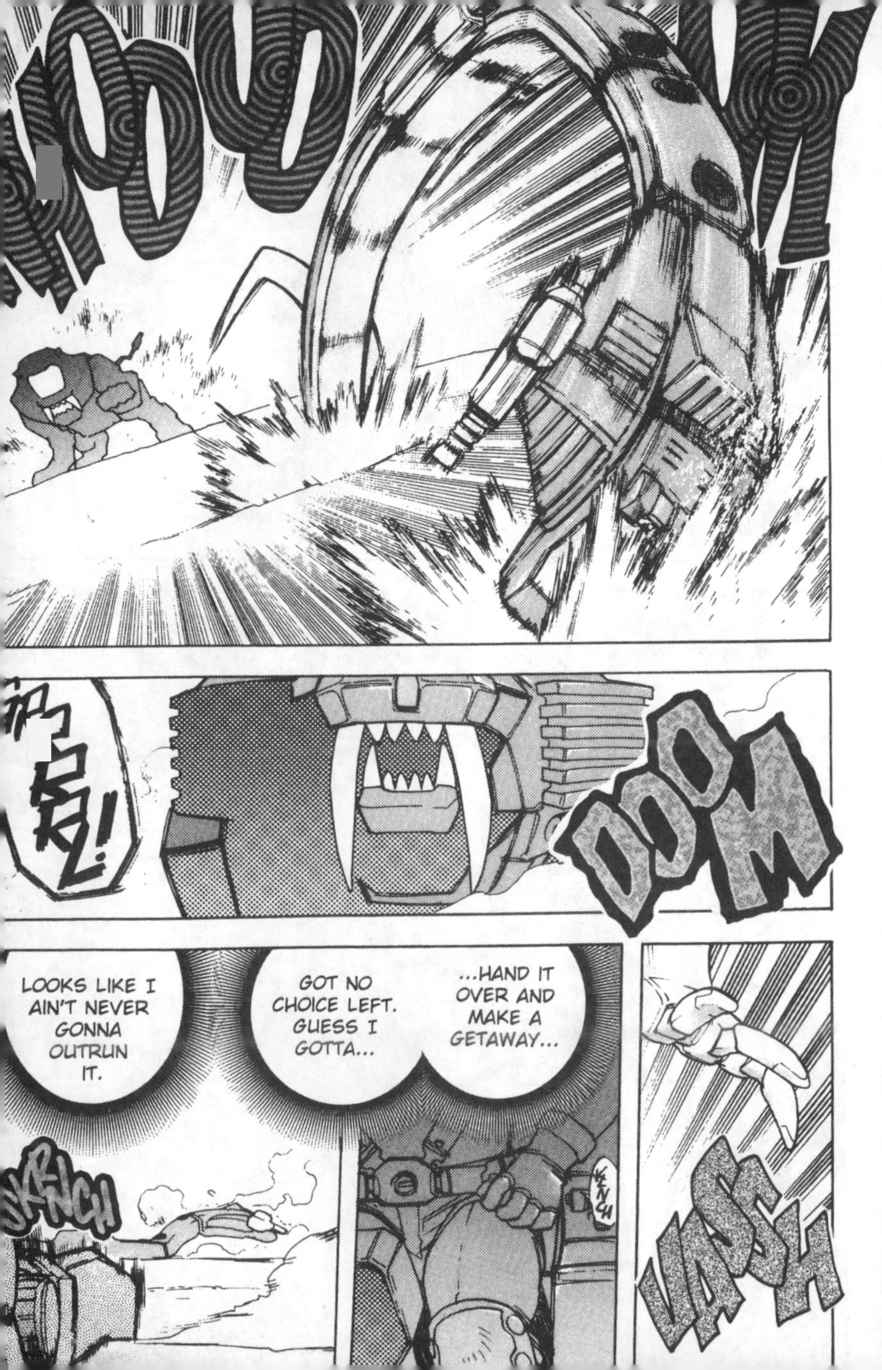
DOOM
LOOKS LIKE I AIN'T NEVER GONNA OUTRUN IT.
GOT NO CHOICE LEFT. GUESS I GOTTA...
...HAND IT OVER AND MAKE A GETAWAY...
WRENCH

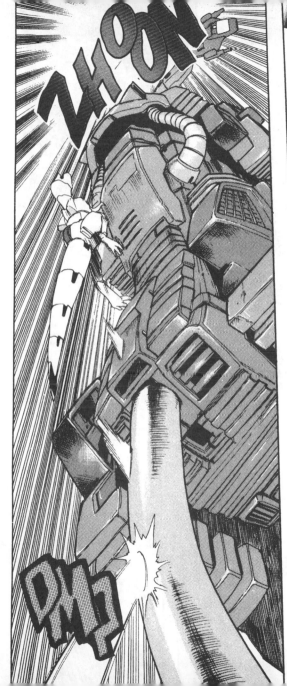

STOP IT! THAT VENOMOUS VIPER'S *MINE!!*

YOU'RE A LATECOMER! NO POACHING!

LET'S SEE WHAT YOU LOOK LIKE!

?!

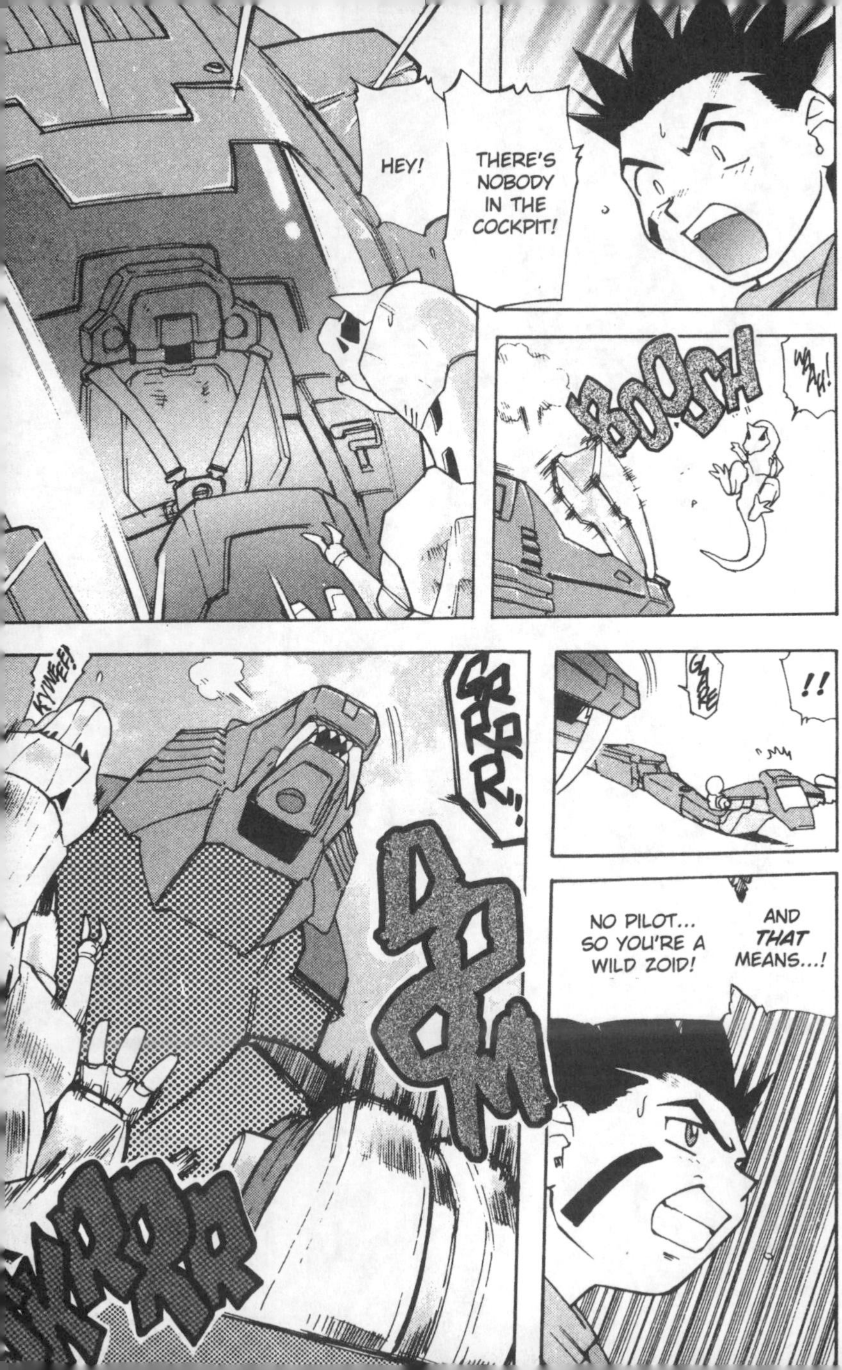
HEY!
THERE'S NOBODY IN THE COCKPIT!
BOOSH
WAAAH!
KYWEE!
GRRRR..!!
WHRRRR
GLARE
!!
NO PILOT... SO YOU'RE A WILD ZOID!
AND *THAT* MEANS...!

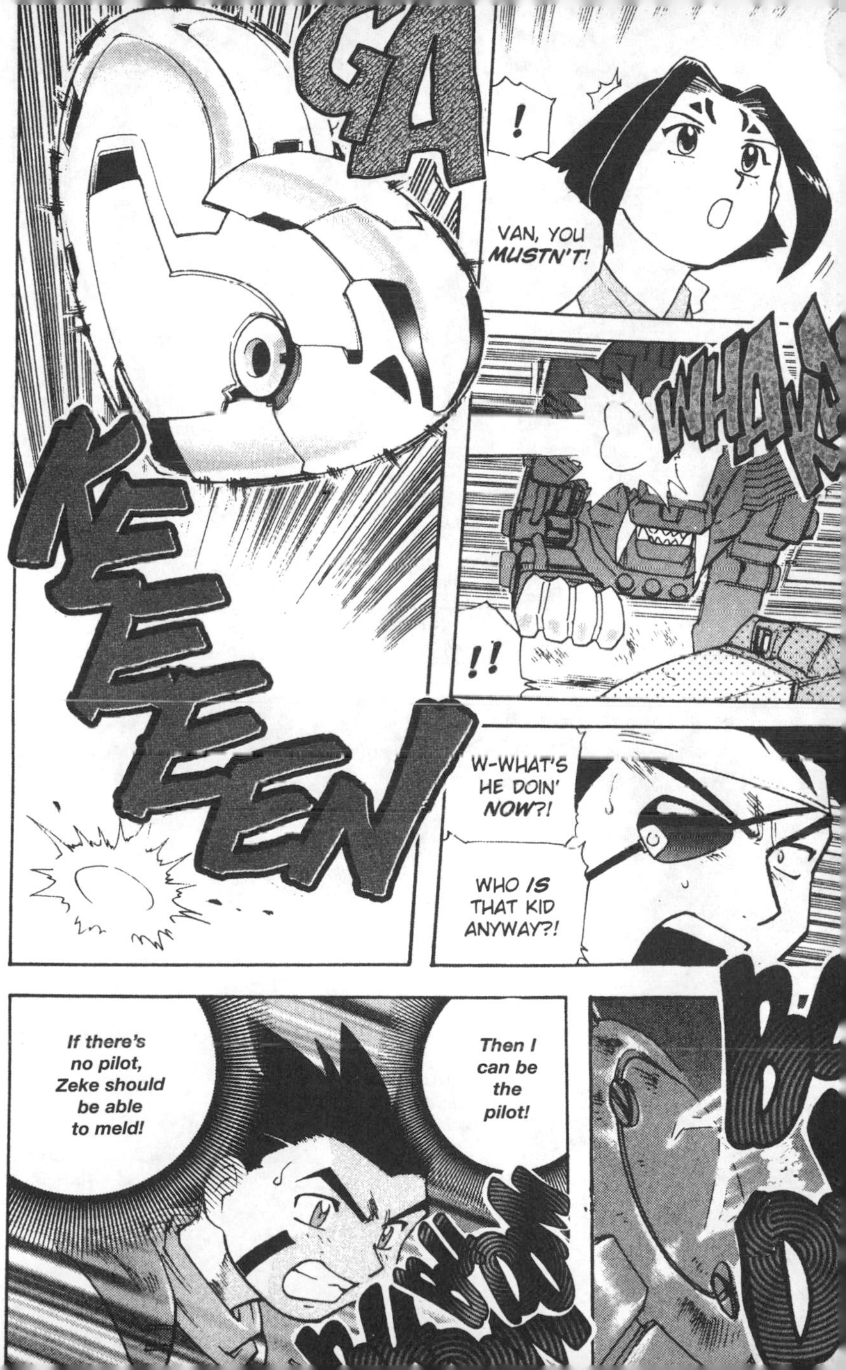
GA
KEEEEEN
!
VAN, YOU MUSTN'T!
!!
W-WHAT'S HE DOIN' NOW?!
WHO IS THAT KID ANYWAY?!
If there's no pilot, Zeke should be able to meld!
Then I can be the pilot!

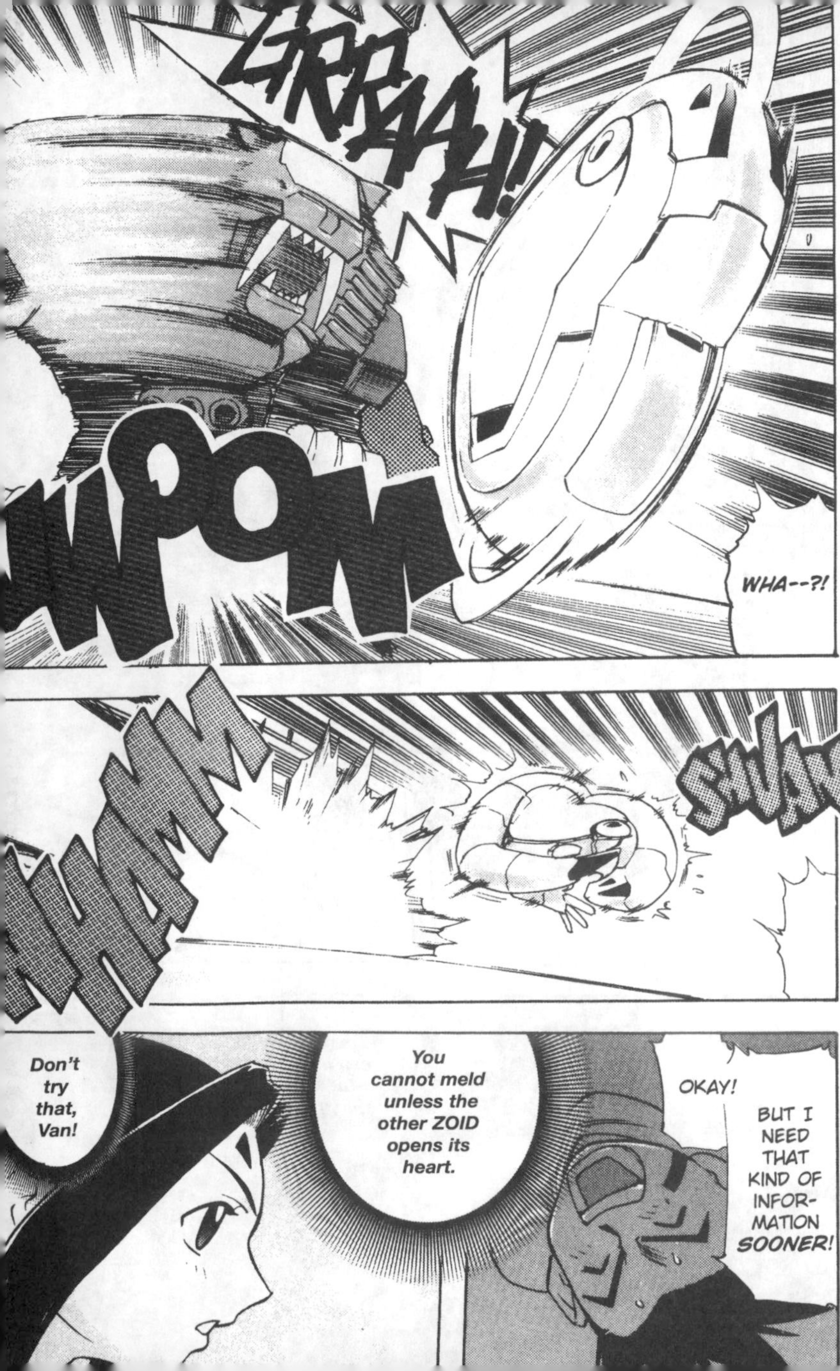
GRRAAH!!
WPOM
WHA--?!
WHAM
SHUM
Don't try that, Van!
You cannot meld unless the other ZOID opens its heart.
OKAY!
BUT I NEED THAT KIND OF INFOR-MATION SOONER!

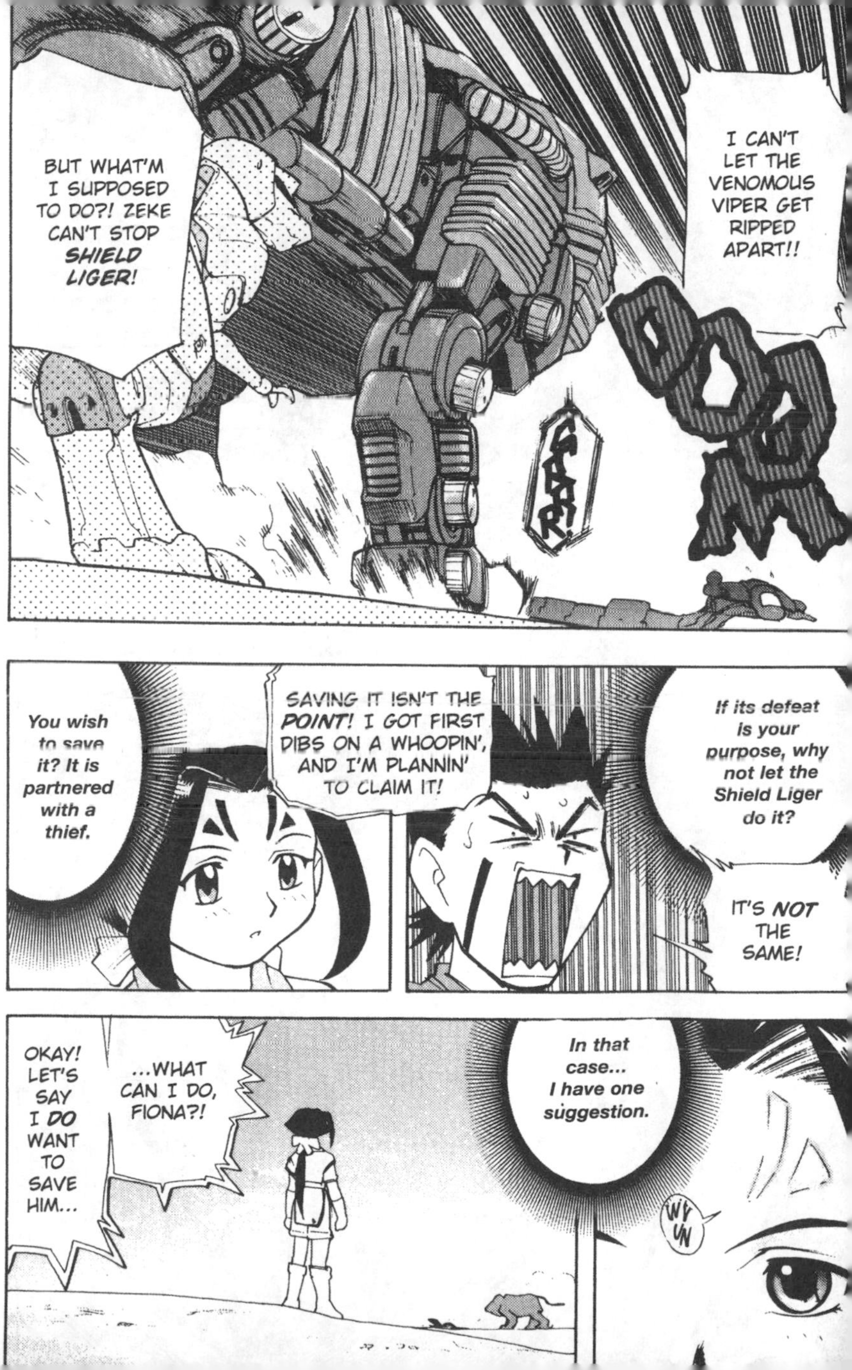
BUT WHAT'M I SUPPOSED TO DO?! ZEKE CAN'T STOP ***SHIELD LIGER***!
GRRR!
I CAN'T LET THE VENOMOUS VIPER GET RIPPED APART!!
DOOM
You wish to save it? It is partnered with a thief.
SAVING IT ISN'T THE ***POINT***! I GOT FIRST DIBS ON A WHOOPIN', AND I'M PLANNIN' TO CLAIM IT!
If its defeat is your purpose, why not let the Shield Liger do it?
IT'S ***NOT*** THE SAME!
OKAY! LET'S SAY I ***DO*** WANT TO SAVE HIM...
...WHAT CAN I DO, FIONA?!
In that case... I have one suggestion.
WYUN

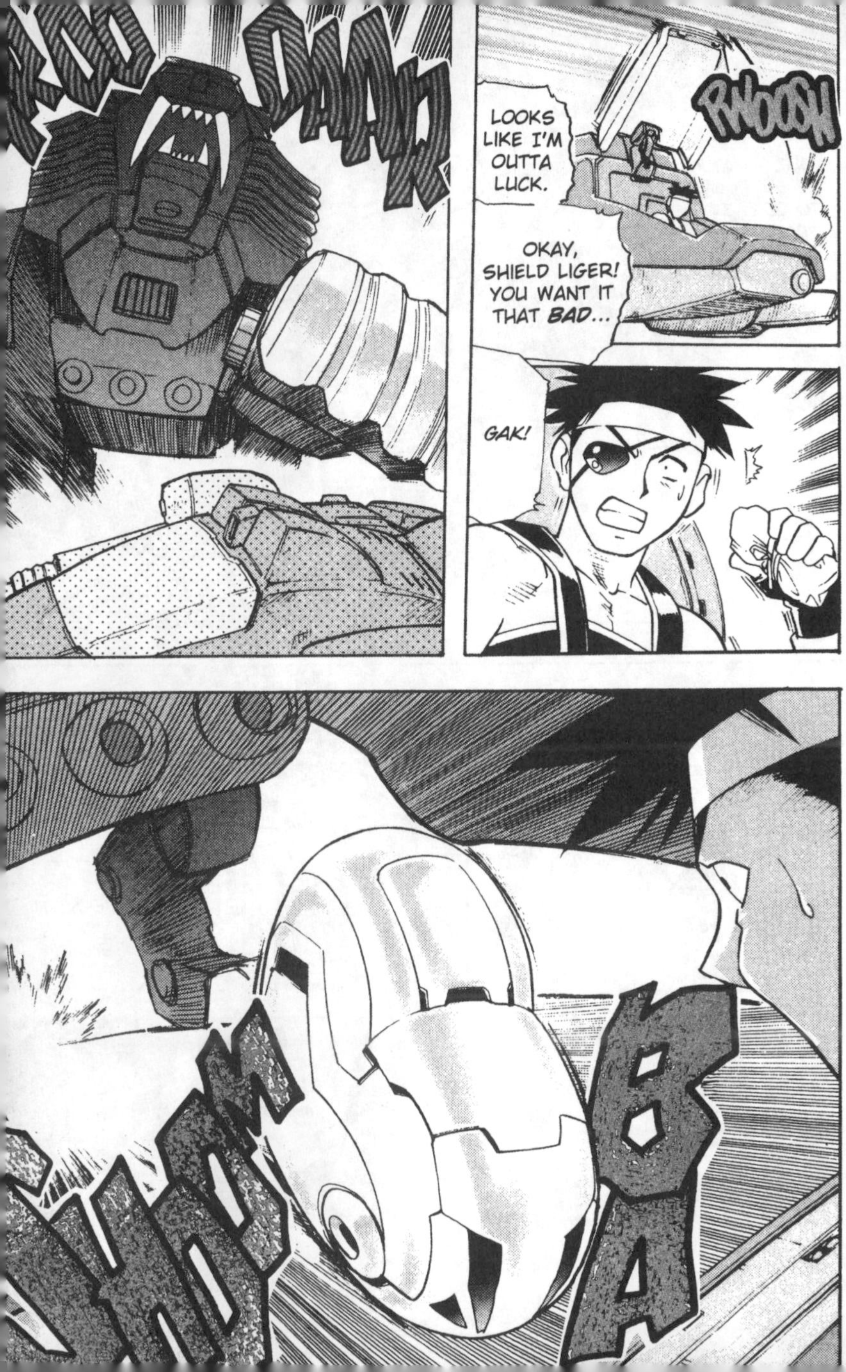

LOOKS LIKE I'M OUTTA LUCK.
RWOOSH
OKAY, SHIELD LIGER! YOU WANT IT THAT *BAD*...
GAK!

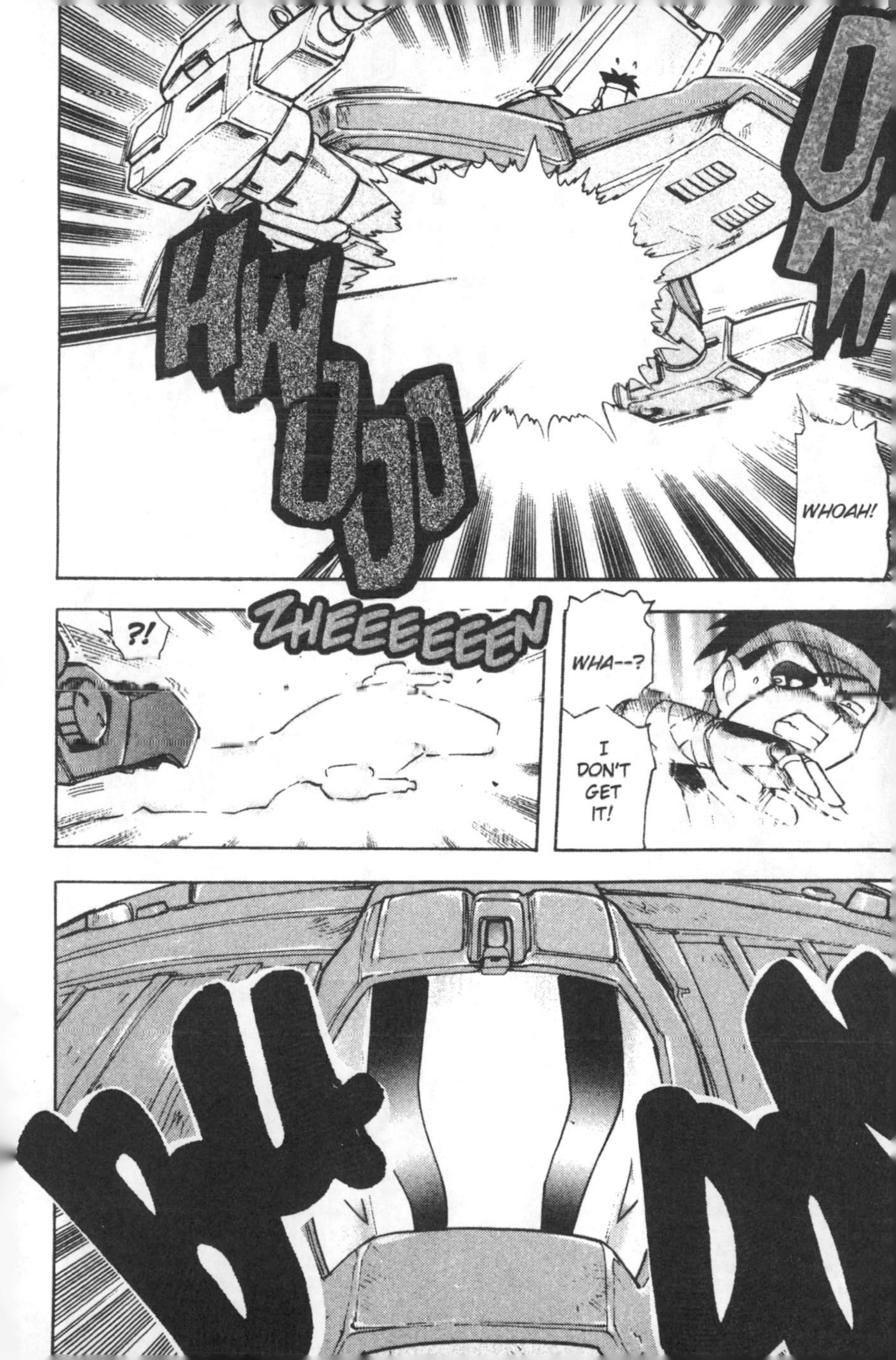
WHOAH!
?!
ZHEEEEEEEN
WHA--?
I DON'T GET IT!

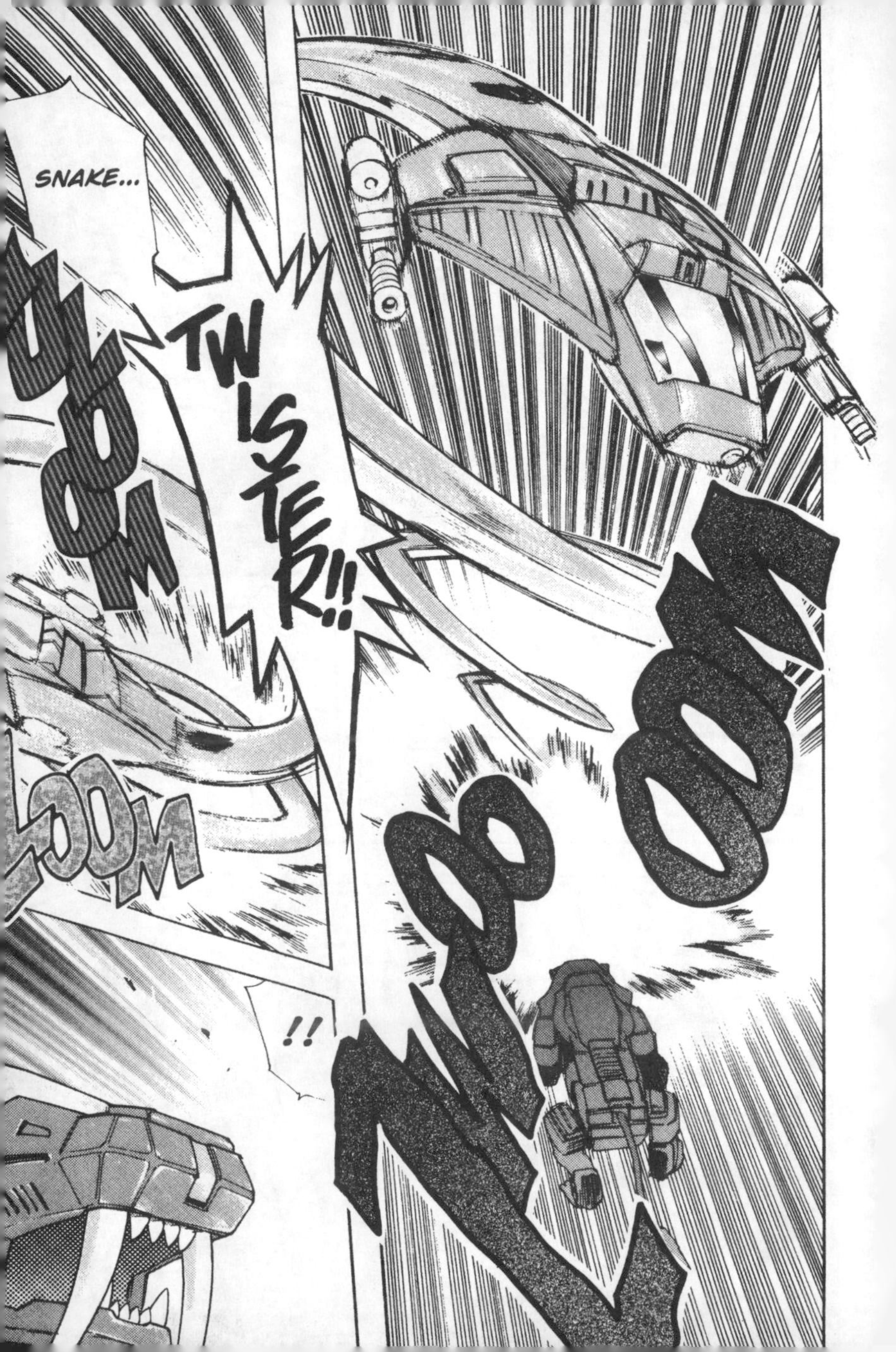
SNAKE...
DOOM
TWISTER!!
ZOOM
!!
ZOOOOM

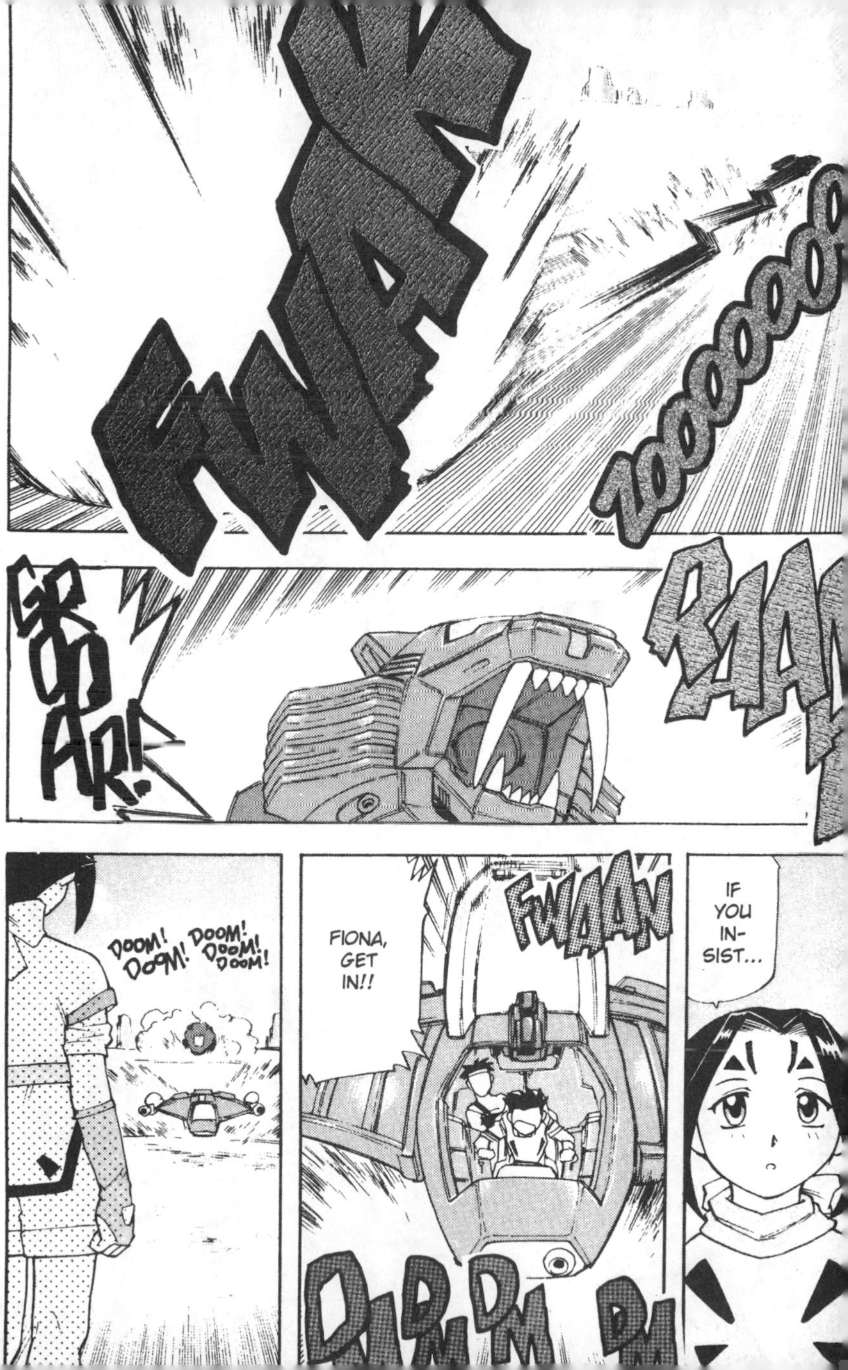

DOOM! DOOM! DOOM! DOOM! DOOM!
FIONA, GET IN!!
FWAAN
IF YOU IN-SIST...

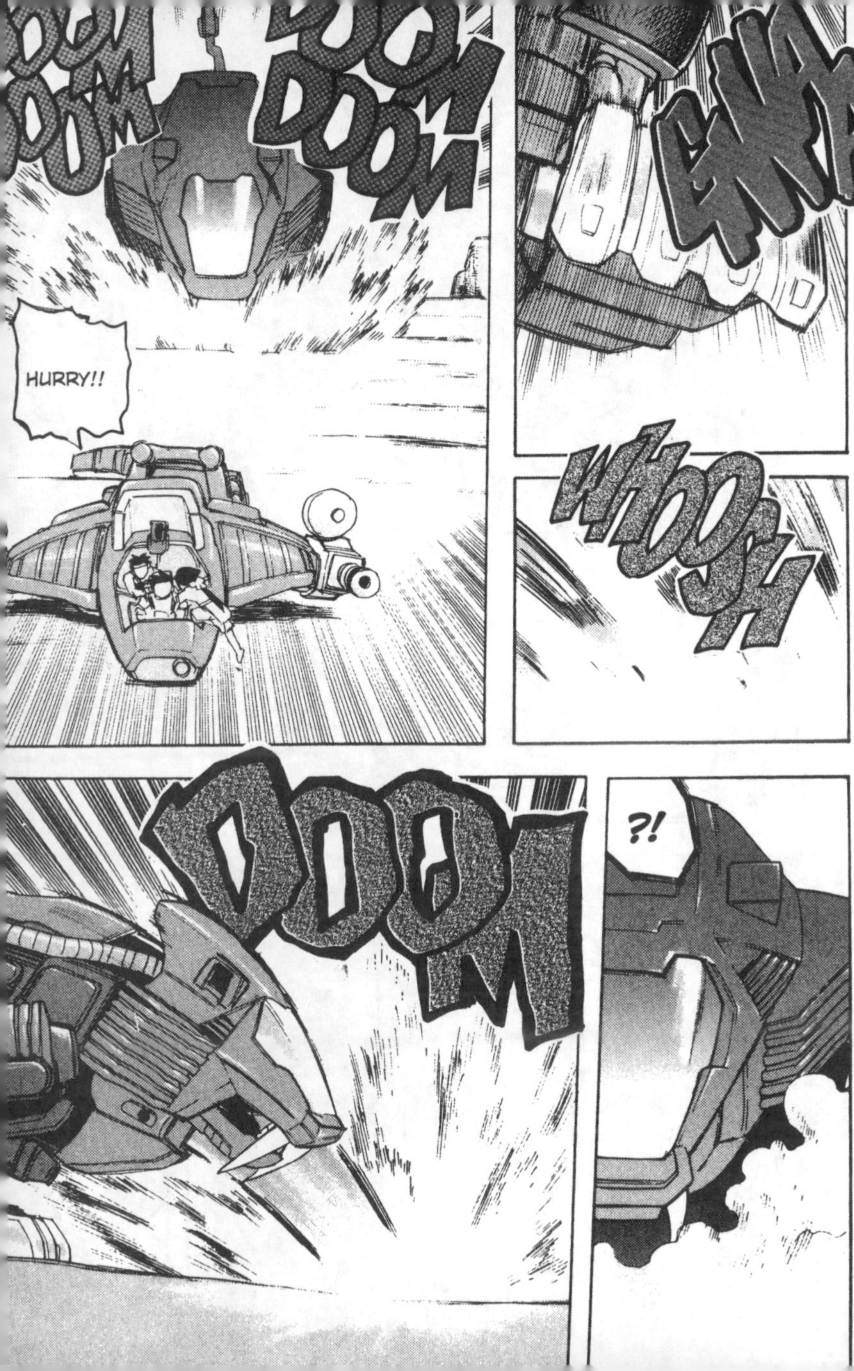
DOOM DOOM
DOOM DOOM
HURRY!!
CHKA
WHOOSH
DOOM
?!

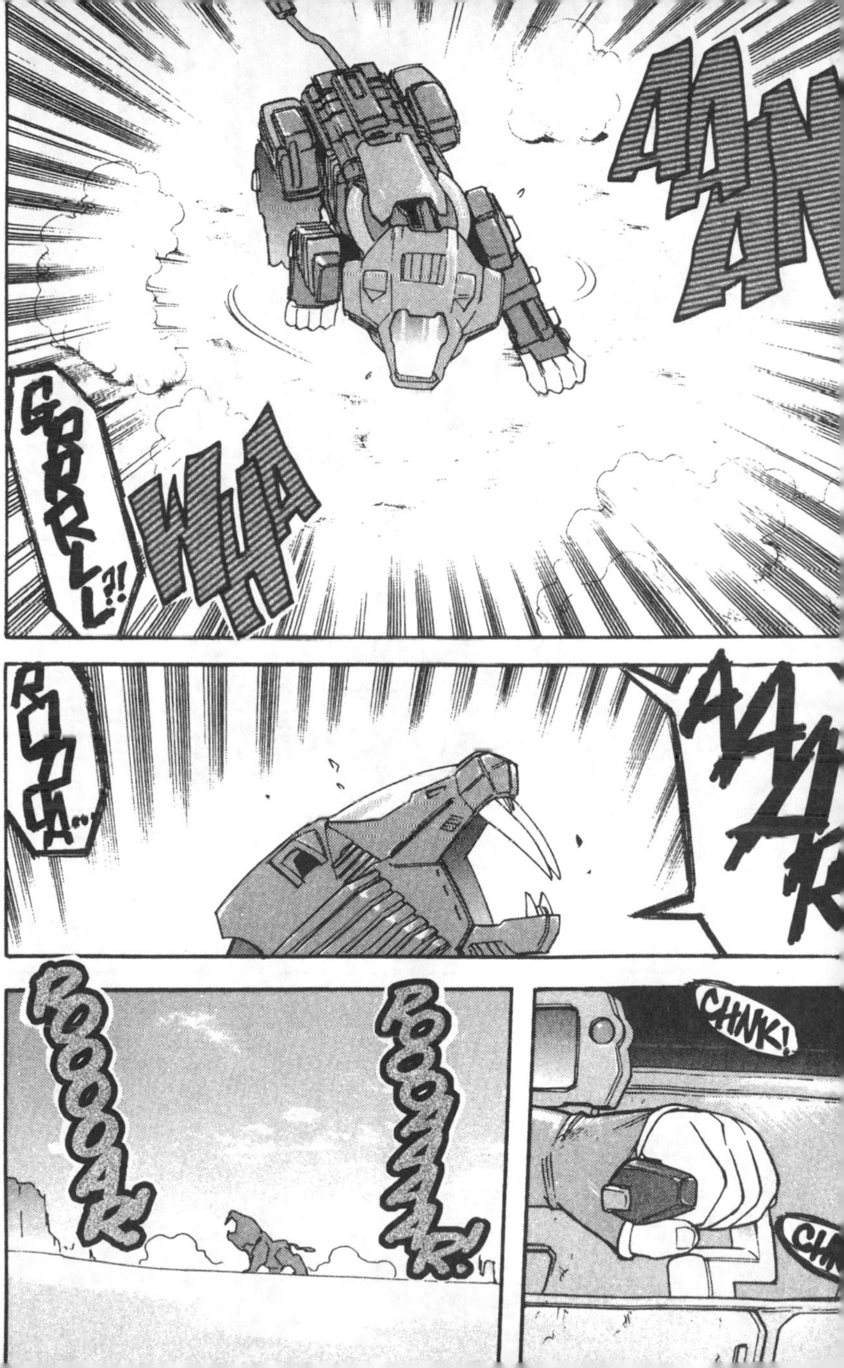
AAAAAN
WHA
GOORRLL?!
AAAAR
ROZCHA...
CHNK!
ROOOOAR
ROOOAAAR!

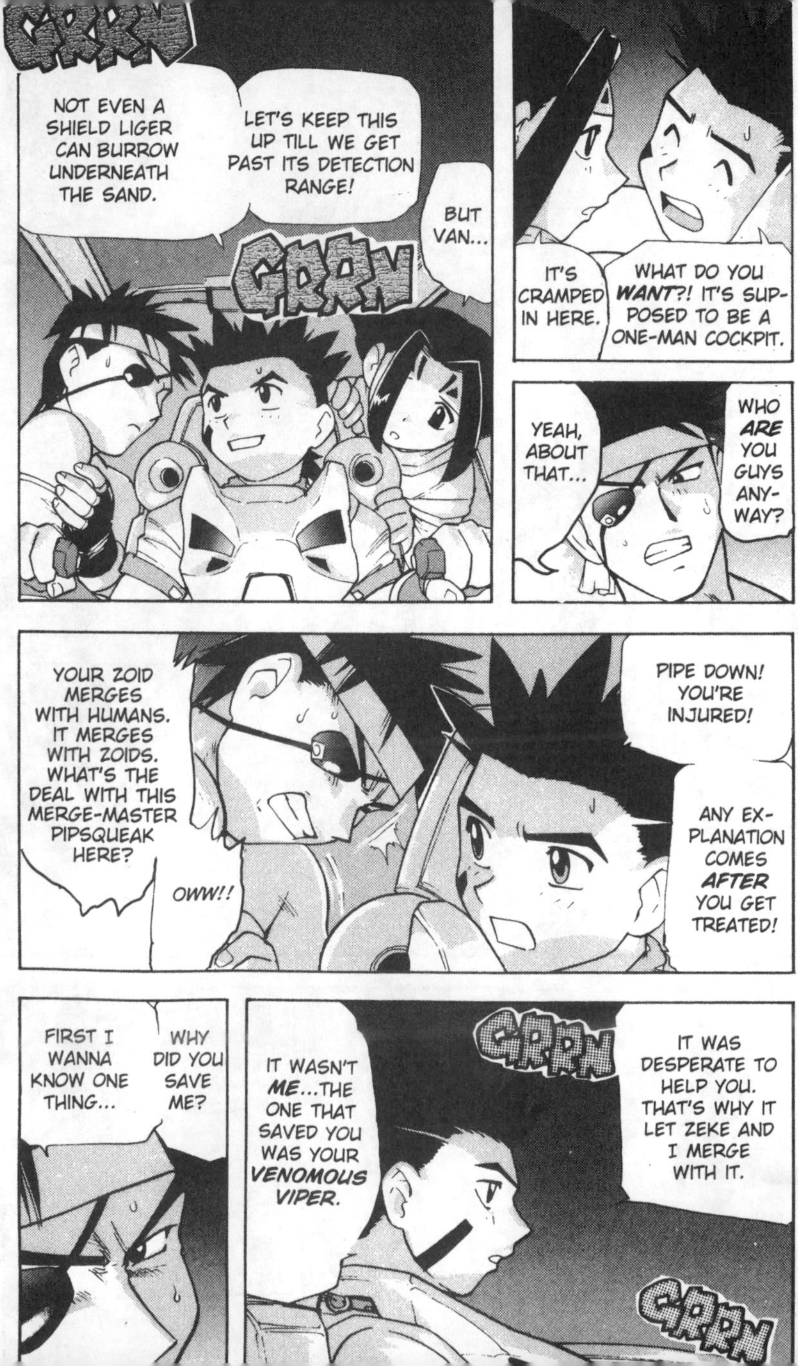
GRRN
NOT EVEN A SHIELD LIGER CAN BURROW UNDERNEATH THE SAND.
LET'S KEEP THIS UP TILL WE GET PAST ITS DETECTION RANGE!
BUT VAN...
GRRN
IT'S CRAMPED IN HERE.
WHAT DO YOU WANT?! IT'S SUPPOSED TO BE A ONE-MAN COCKPIT.
YEAH, ABOUT THAT...
WHO ARE YOU GUYS ANYWAY?
YOUR ZOID MERGES WITH HUMANS. IT MERGES WITH ZOIDS. WHAT'S THE DEAL WITH THIS MERGE-MASTER PIPSQUEAK HERE?
OWW!!
PIPE DOWN! YOU'RE INJURED!
ANY EXPLANATION COMES AFTER YOU GET TREATED!
FIRST I WANNA KNOW ONE THING...
WHY DID YOU SAVE ME?
IT WASN'T ME...THE ONE THAT SAVED YOU WAS YOUR VENOMOUS VIPER.
GRRN
IT WAS DESPERATE TO HELP YOU. THAT'S WHY IT LET ZEKE AND I MERGE WITH IT.
GRRN

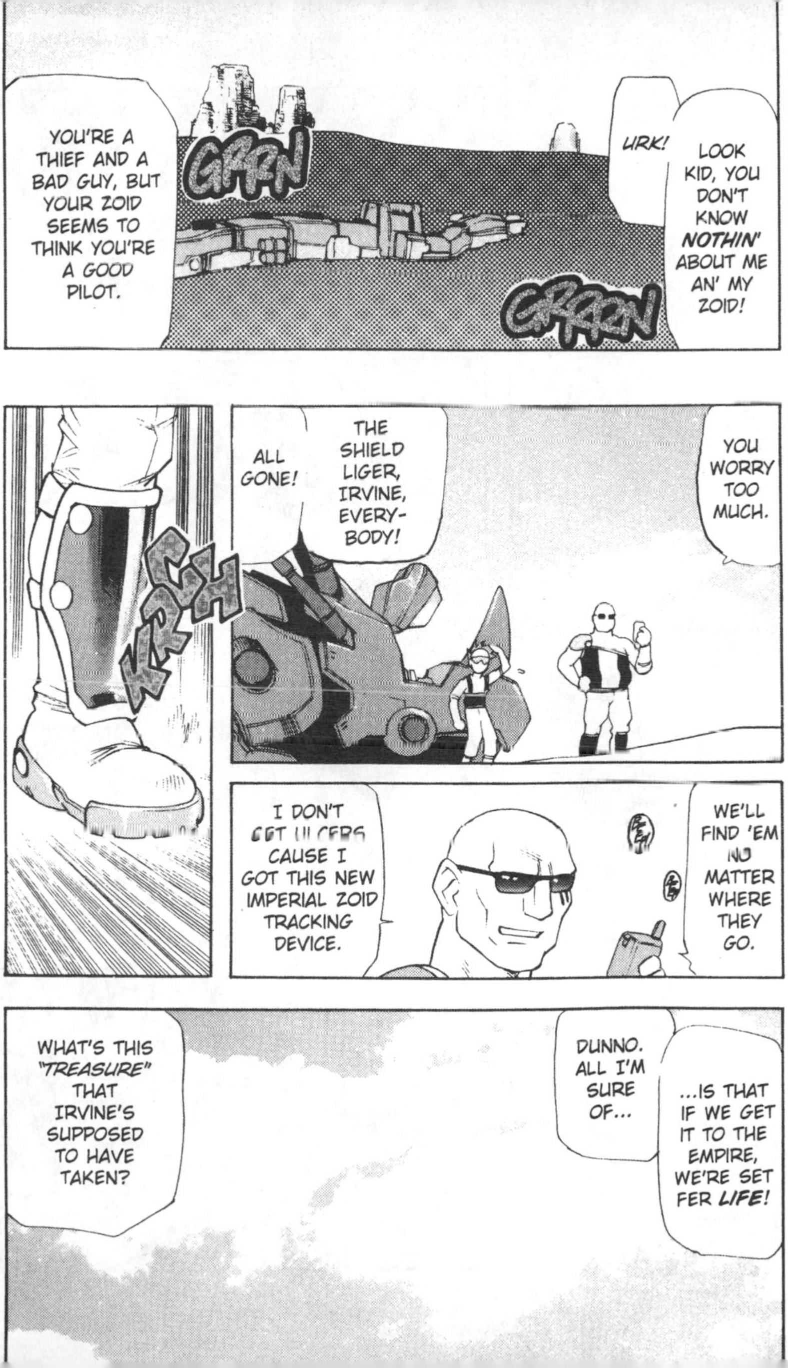

YOU'RE A THIEF AND A BAD GUY, BUT YOUR ZOID SEEMS TO THINK YOU'RE A GOOD PILOT.
GRRN
GRRRN
URK!
LOOK KID, YOU DON'T KNOW *NOTHIN'* ABOUT ME AN' MY ZOID!
KRSH
ALL GONE!
THE SHIELD LIGER, IRVINE, EVERY-BODY!
YOU WORRY TOO MUCH.
I DON'T GET ULCERS CAUSE I GOT THIS NEW IMPERIAL ZOID TRACKING DEVICE.
WE'LL FIND 'EM NO MATTER WHERE THEY GO.
WHAT'S THIS *"TREASURE"* THAT IRVINE'S SUPPOSED TO HAVE TAKEN?
DUNNO. ALL I'M SURE OF...
...IS THAT IF WE GET IT TO THE EMPIRE, WE'RE SET FER *LIFE*!

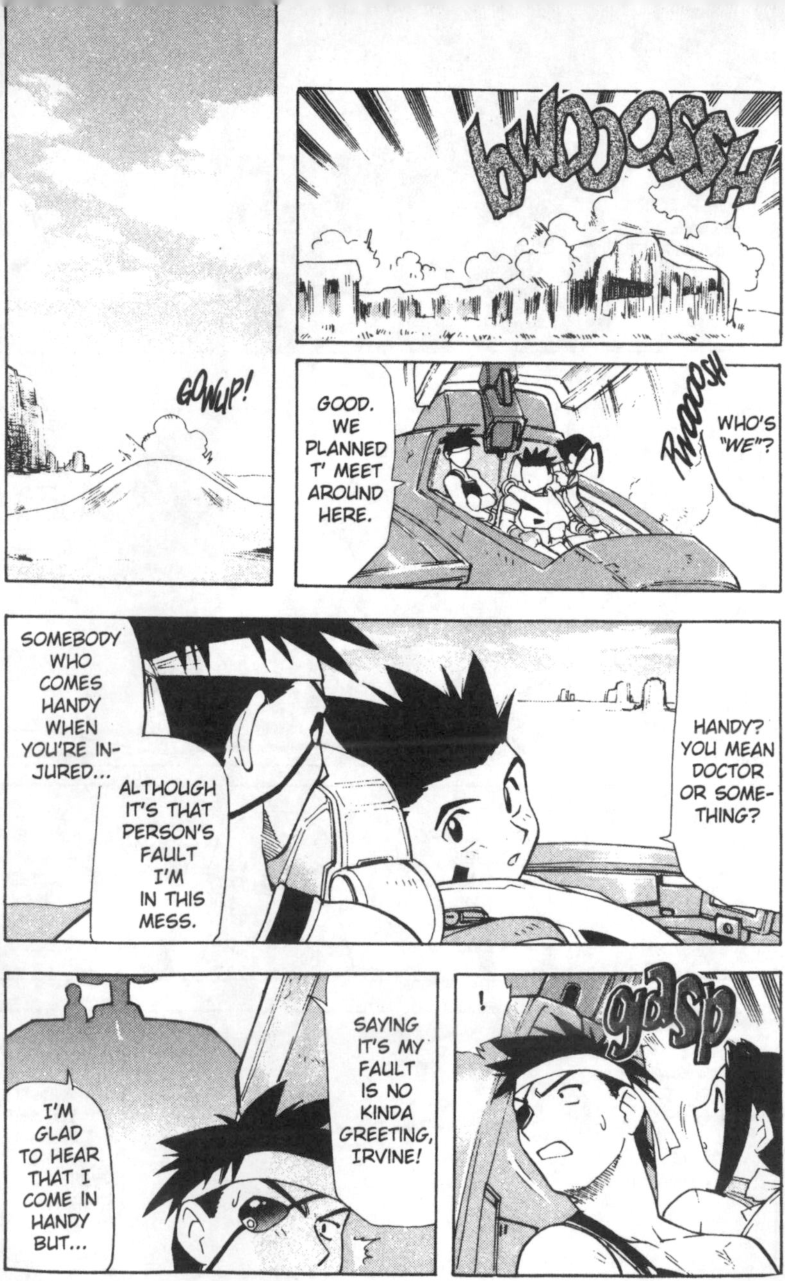

BWOOOSH
GOWUP!
GOOD. WE PLANNED T' MEET AROUND HERE.
RWOOOSH
WHO'S "WE"?
SOMEBODY WHO COMES HANDY WHEN YOU'RE IN-JURED...
ALTHOUGH IT'S THAT PERSON'S FAULT I'M IN THIS MESS.
HANDY? YOU MEAN DOCTOR OR SOME-THING?
I'M GLAD TO HEAR THAT I COME IN HANDY BUT...
SAYING IT'S MY FAULT IS NO KINDA GREETING, IRVINE!
!
GRASP

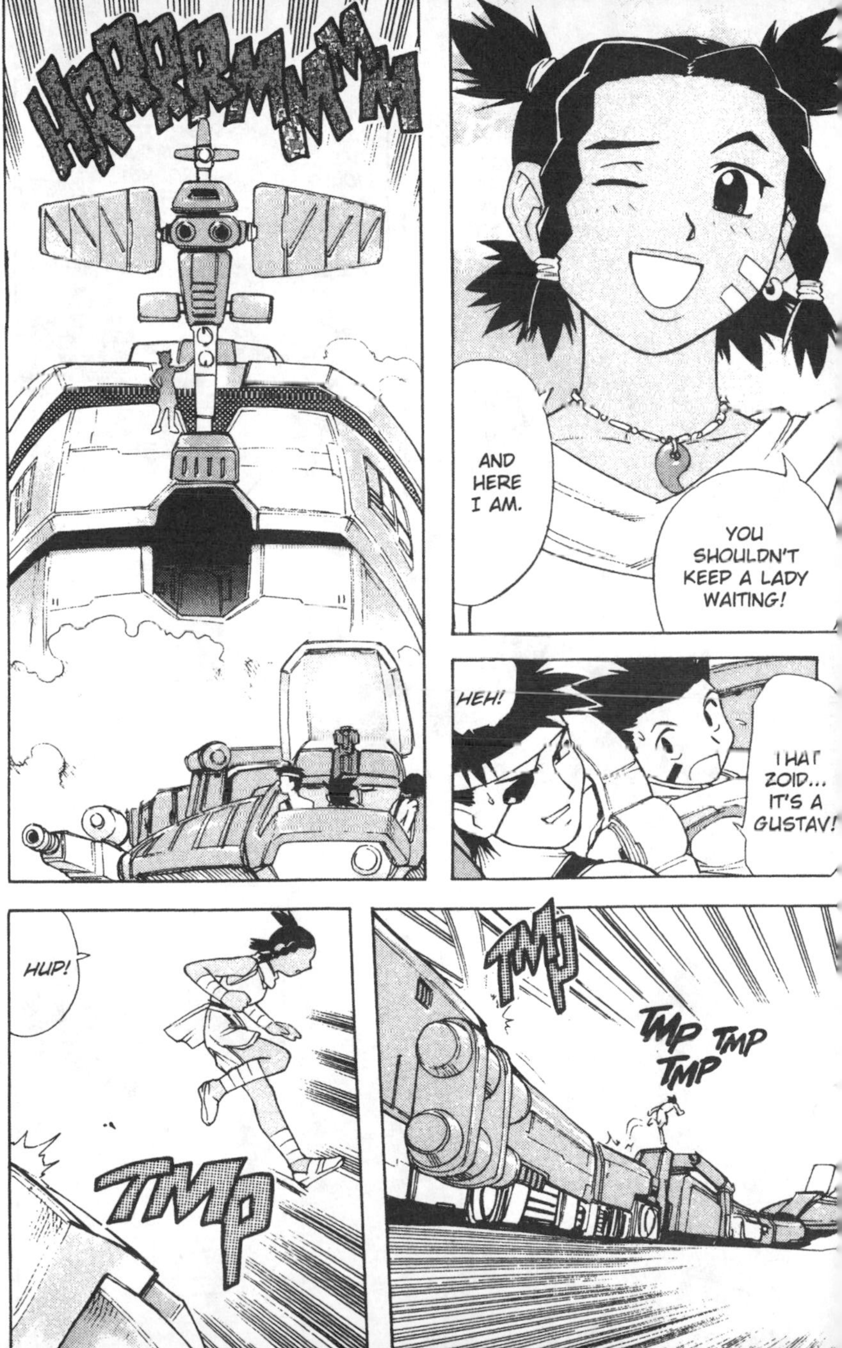
HRRRRMMMMM
AND HERE I AM.
YOU SHOULDN'T KEEP A LADY WAITING!
HEH!
THAT ZOID... IT'S A GUSTAV!
HUP!
TMP
TMP
TMP TMP
TMP

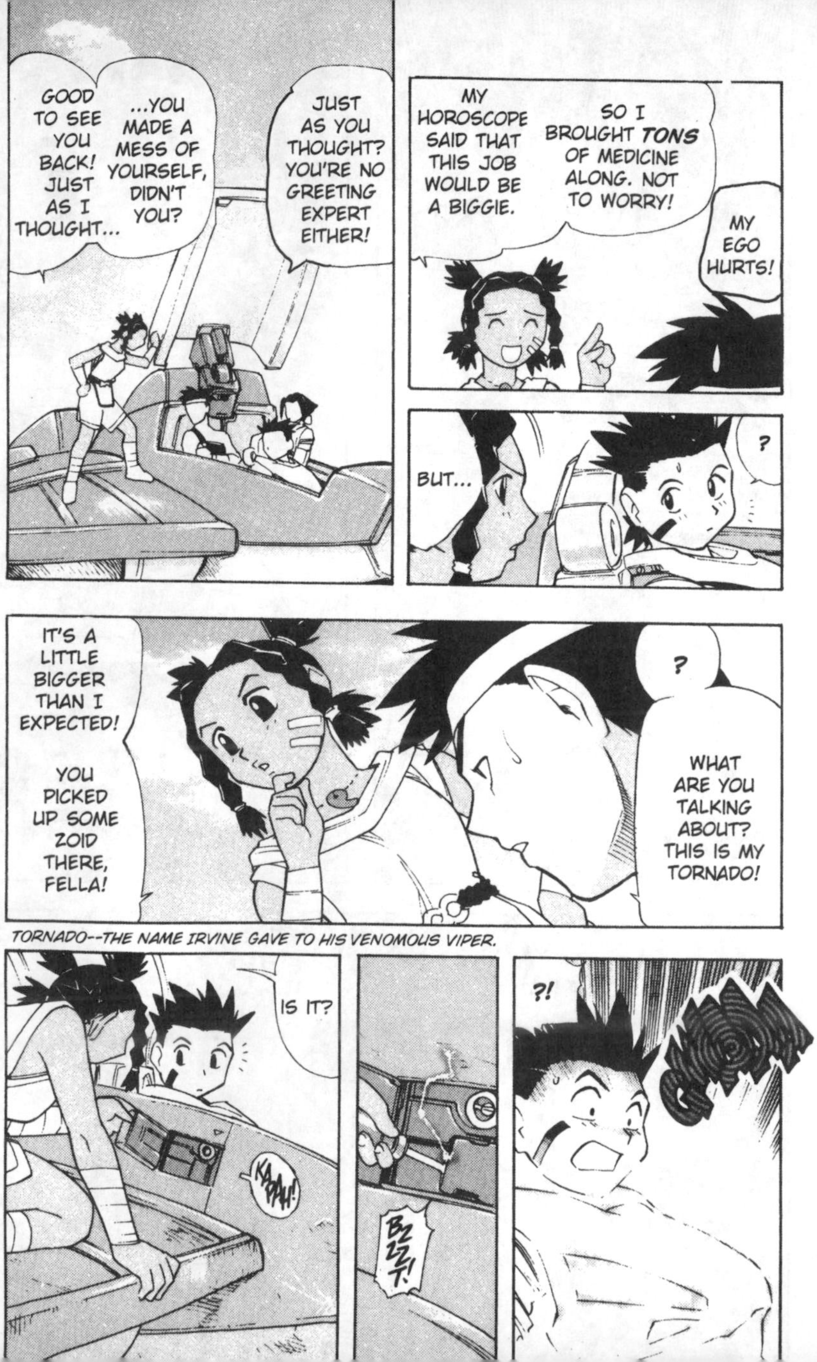
GOOD TO SEE YOU BACK! JUST AS I THOUGHT...
...YOU MADE A MESS OF YOURSELF, DIDN'T YOU?
JUST AS YOU THOUGHT? YOU'RE NO GREETING EXPERT EITHER!
MY HOROSCOPE SAID THAT THIS JOB WOULD BE A BIGGIE.
SO I BROUGHT **TONS** OF MEDICINE ALONG. NOT TO WORRY!
MY EGO HURTS!
BUT...
?
IT'S A LITTLE BIGGER THAN I EXPECTED!
YOU PICKED UP SOME ZOID THERE, FELLA!
?
WHAT ARE YOU TALKING ABOUT? THIS IS MY TORNADO!
TORNADO--THE NAME IRVINE GAVE TO HIS VENOMOUS VIPER.
IS IT?
KAPAH!
BZZZT!
?!

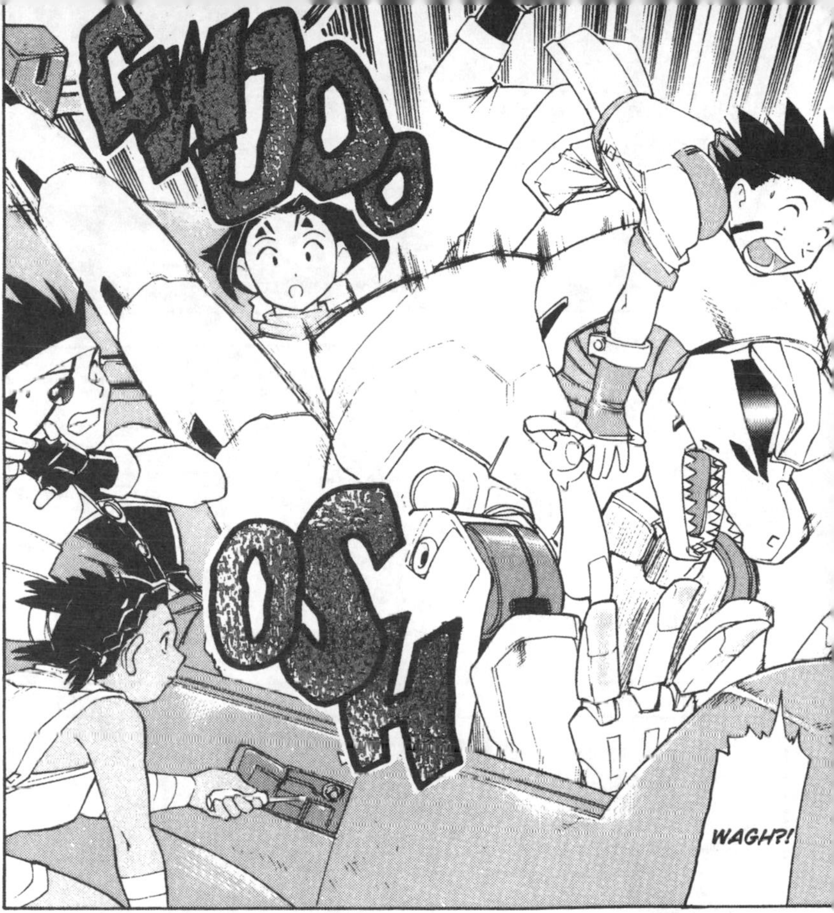
WAGH?!

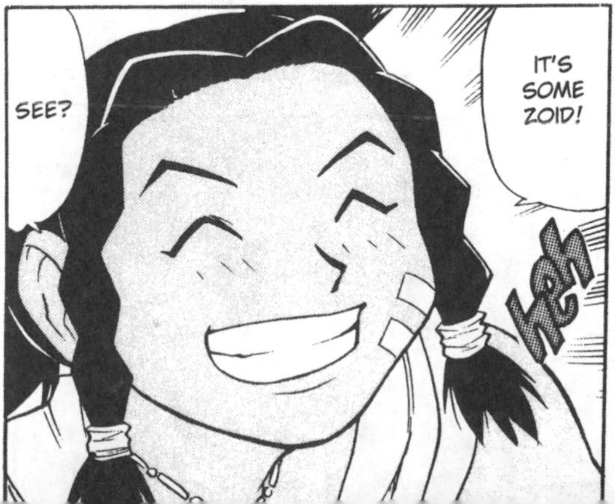
SEE?
IT'S SOME ZOID!
heh

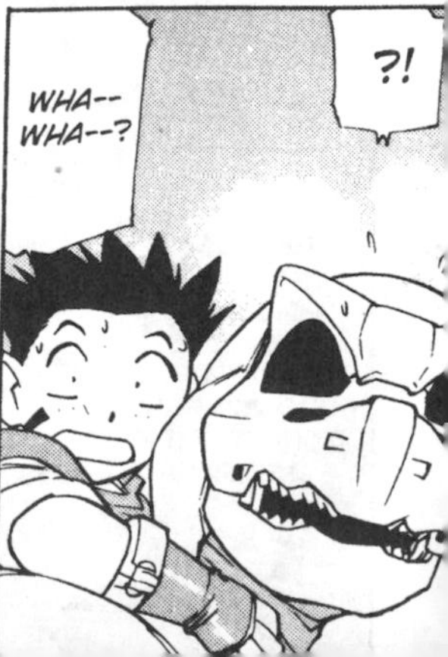
WHA-- WHA--?
?!

RRR...

GRNN!!

ANY **MAN** SHOULD BE ABLE TO TAKE THAT KIND OF HEAT.

AWW SHADDAP!

WHAT KINDA TREATMENT IS THAT?

IT'S MOXIBUSTION! YOU STIMULATE THE BODY'S PRESSURE POINTS, AND IT MAKES THE BODY'S ENERGIES FLOW, ACCELERATING THE HEALING.

THE FLOW OF ENERGIES...?

YOU'VE ALREADY SEEN IT WORK. I POKED THE VENOMOUS VIPER'S PRESSURE POINT AND DISRUPTED ITS ENERGIES.

THAT'S WHY YOU COULDN'T HOLD THE MERGE!

WHO...

...ARE YOU?

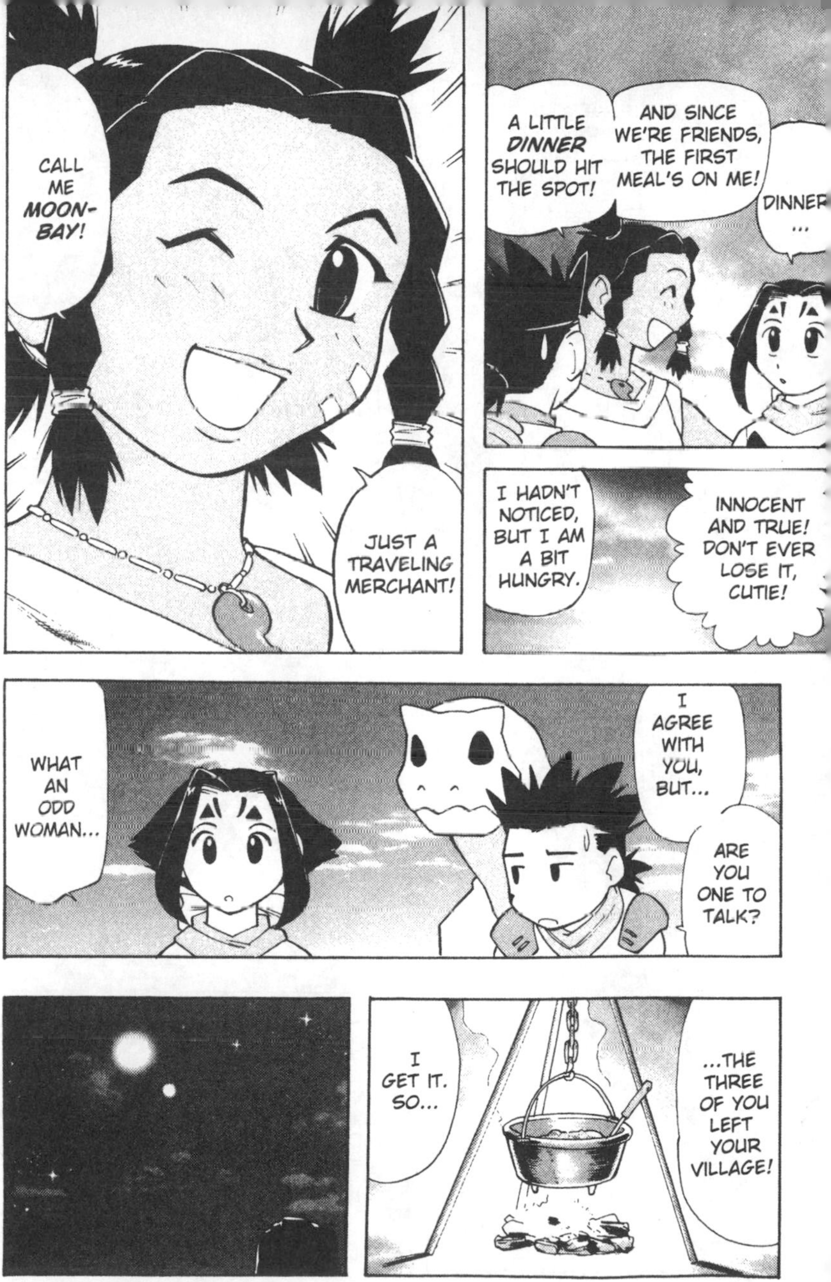
CALL ME MOON-BAY!
JUST A TRAVELING MERCHANT!
A LITTLE DINNER SHOULD HIT THE SPOT!
AND SINCE WE'RE FRIENDS, THE FIRST MEAL'S ON ME!
DINNER ...
I HADN'T NOTICED, BUT I AM A BIT HUNGRY.
INNOCENT AND TRUE! DON'T EVER LOSE IT, CUTIE!
WHAT AN ODD WOMAN...
I AGREE WITH YOU, BUT...
ARE YOU ONE TO TALK?
I GET IT. SO...
...THE THREE OF YOU LEFT YOUR VILLAGE!

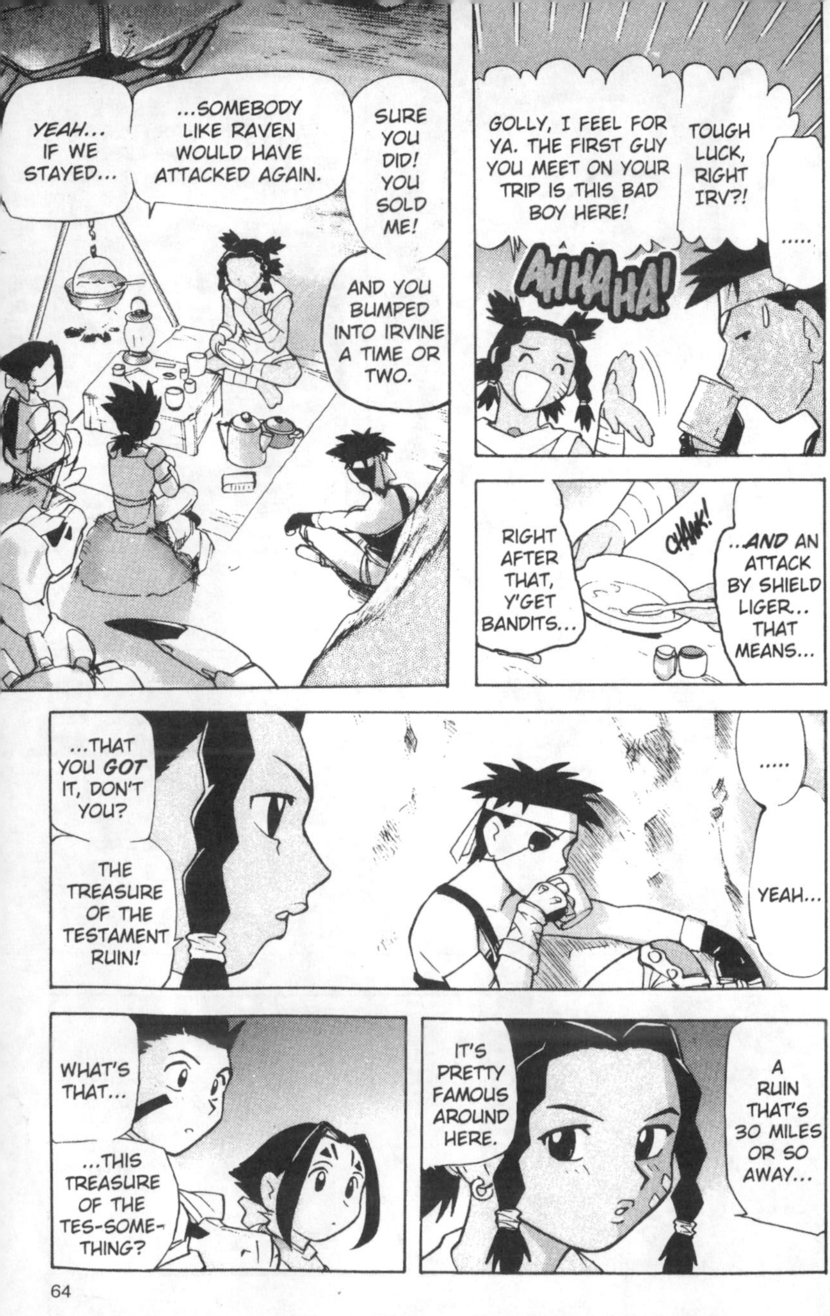
YEAH... IF WE STAYED...
...SOMEBODY LIKE RAVEN WOULD HAVE ATTACKED AGAIN.
SURE YOU DID! YOU SOLD ME!
AND YOU BUMPED INTO IRVINE A TIME OR TWO.
GOLLY, I FEEL FOR YA. THE FIRST GUY YOU MEET ON YOUR TRIP IS THIS BAD BOY HERE!
AHHAHA!
TOUGH LUCK, RIGHT IRV?!
.....
RIGHT AFTER THAT, Y'GET BANDITS...
CHANK!
...AND AN ATTACK BY SHIELD LIGER... THAT MEANS...
...THAT YOU GOT IT, DON'T YOU?
THE TREASURE OF THE TESTAMENT RUIN!
.....
YEAH...
WHAT'S THAT...
...THIS TREASURE OF THE TES-SOME-THING?
IT'S PRETTY FAMOUS AROUND HERE.
A RUIN THAT'S 30 MILES OR SO AWAY...

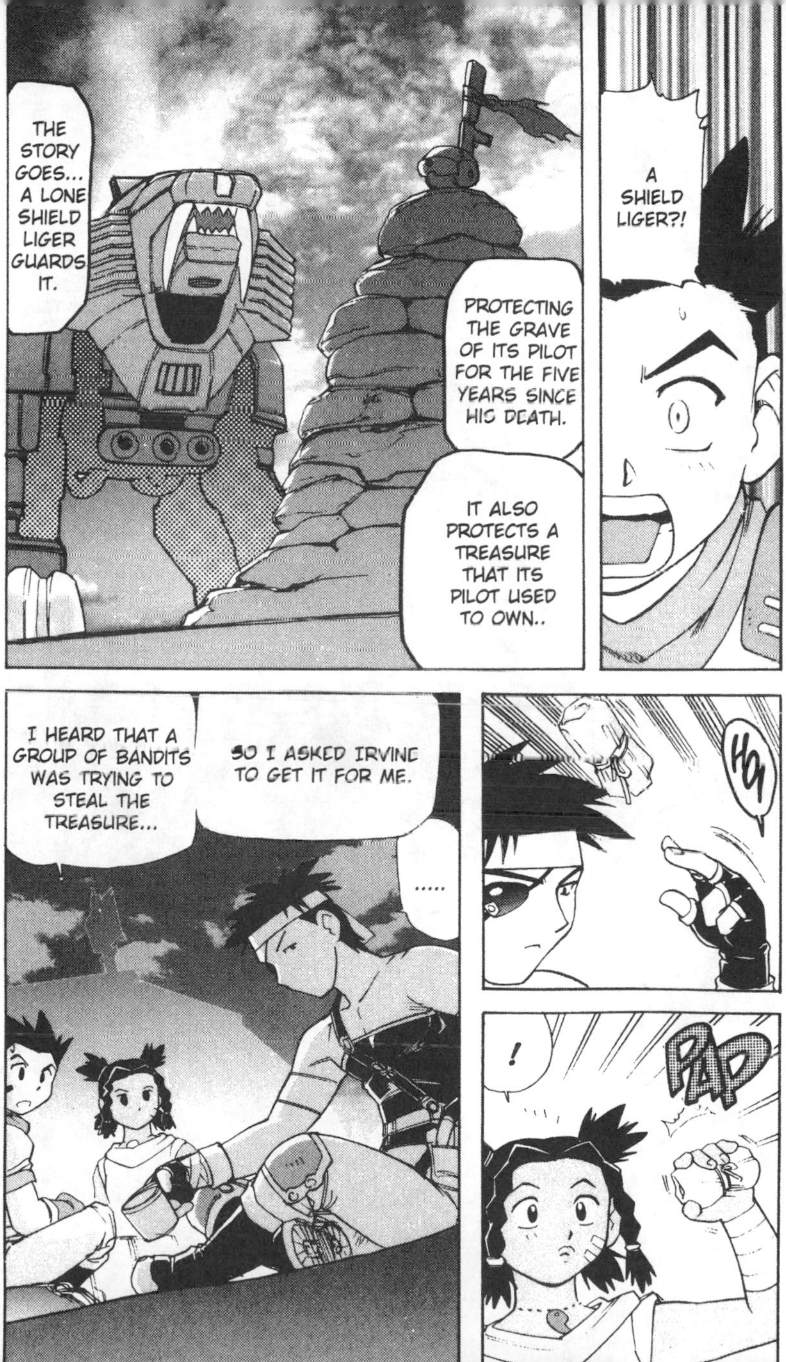
THE STORY GOES... A LONE SHIELD LIGER GUARDS IT.
PROTECTING THE GRAVE OF ITS PILOT FOR THE FIVE YEARS SINCE HIS DEATH.
IT ALSO PROTECTS A TREASURE THAT ITS PILOT USED TO OWN..
A SHIELD LIGER?!
I HEARD THAT A GROUP OF BANDITS WAS TRYING TO STEAL THE TREASURE...
SO I ASKED IRVINE TO GET IT FOR ME.
.....
HOI
!
PAP

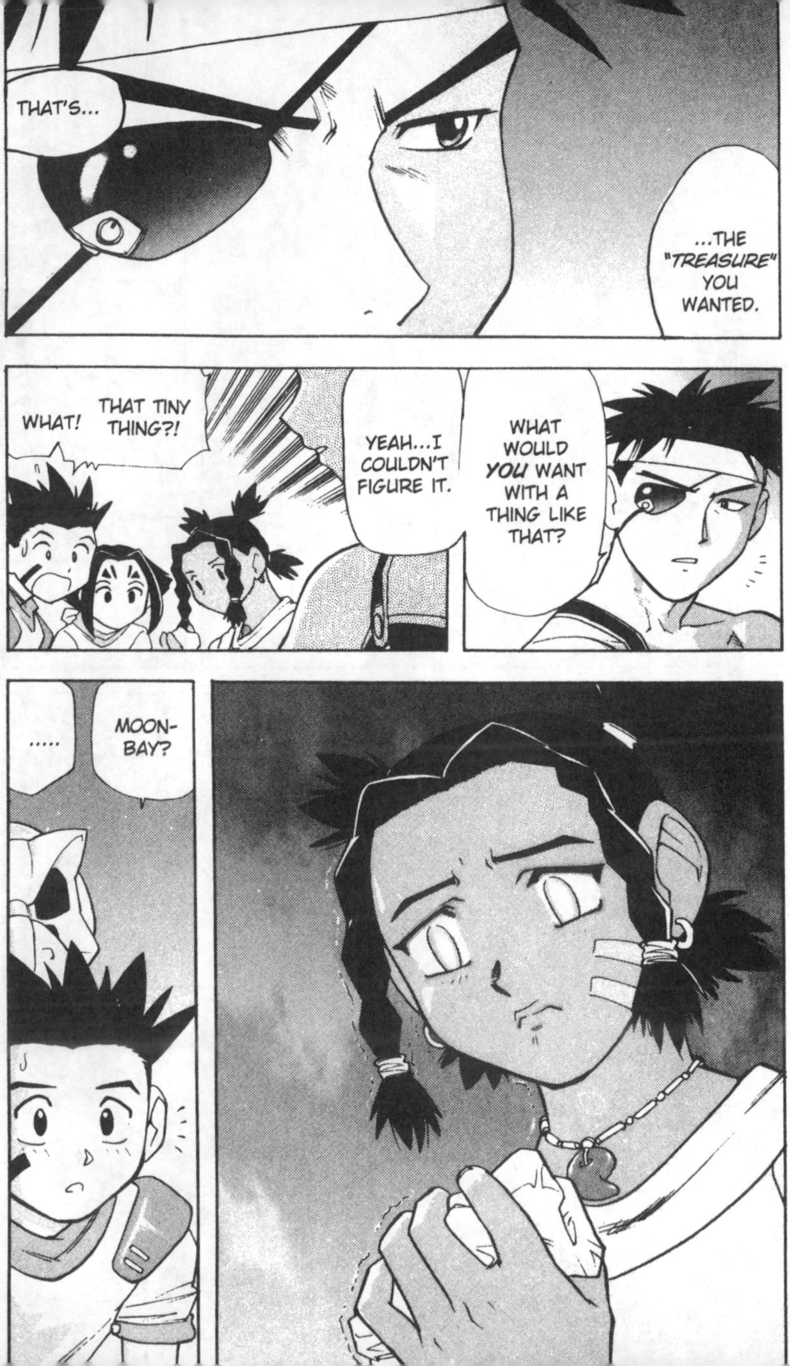
THAT'S...
...THE "*TREASURE*" YOU WANTED.
WHAT!
THAT TINY THING?!
YEAH...I COULDN'T FIGURE IT.
WHAT WOULD *YOU* WANT WITH A THING LIKE THAT?
.....
MOON-BAY?

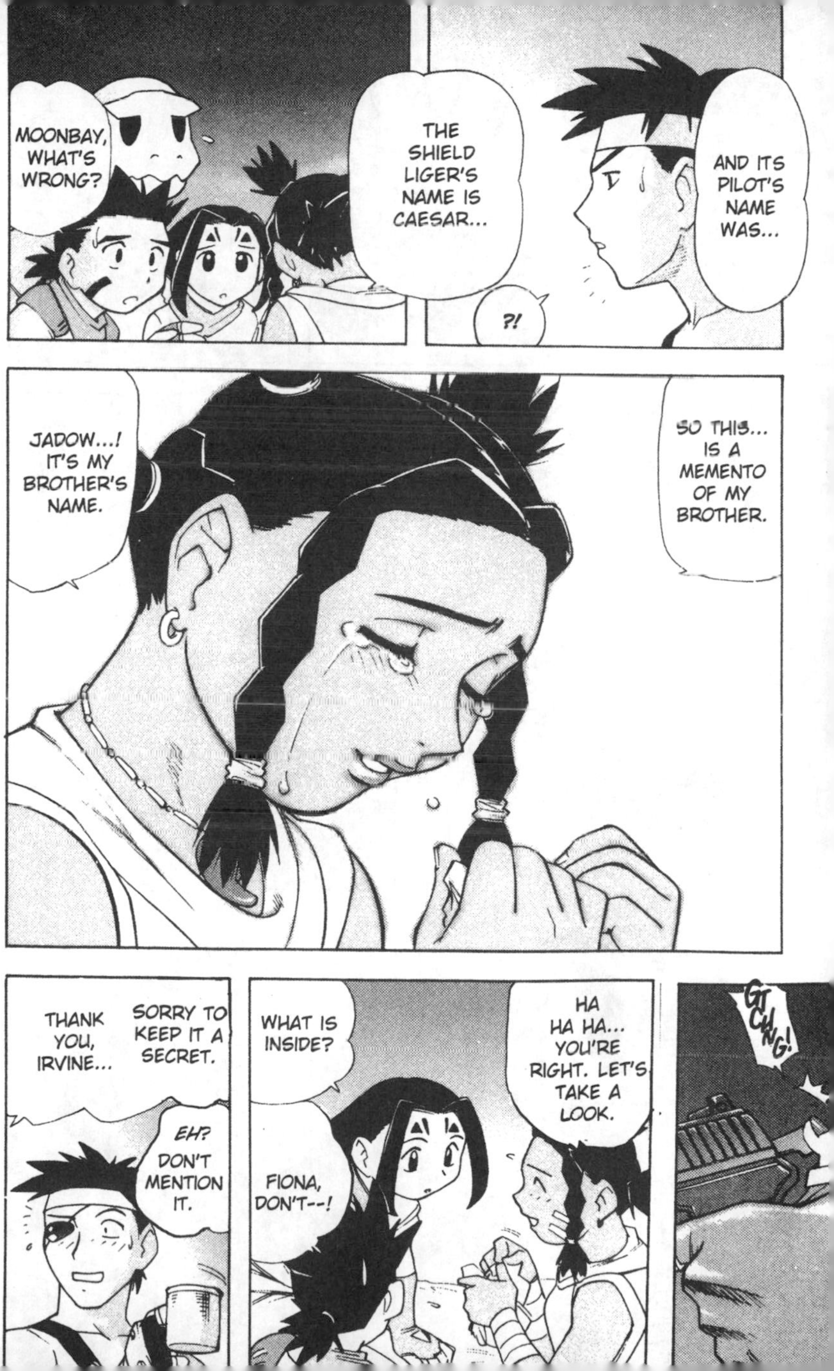
MOONBAY, WHAT'S WRONG?
THE SHIELD LIGER'S NAME IS CAESAR...
AND ITS PILOT'S NAME WAS...
?!
JADOW...! IT'S MY BROTHER'S NAME.
SO THIS... IS A MEMENTO OF MY BROTHER.
THANK YOU, IRVINE...
SORRY TO KEEP IT A SECRET.
EH? DON'T MENTION IT.
WHAT IS INSIDE?
HA HA HA... YOU'RE RIGHT. LET'S TAKE A LOOK.
FIONA, DON'T--!
GTCHNG!

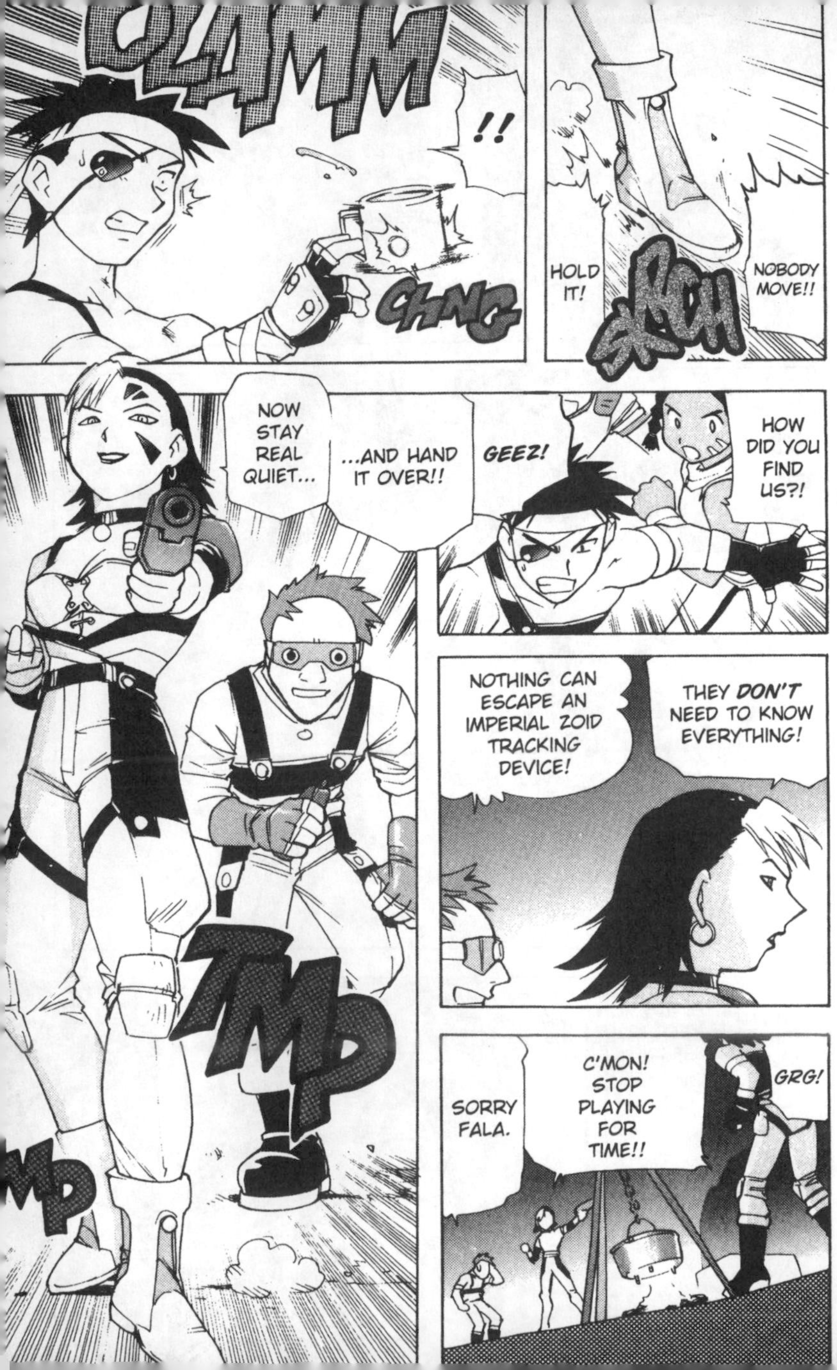
CLAMM
!!
CHNG
HOLD IT!
SKRCH
NOBODY MOVE!!
NOW STAY REAL QUIET...
...AND HAND IT OVER!!
TMP
MP
GEEZ!
HOW DID YOU FIND US?!
NOTHING CAN ESCAPE AN IMPERIAL ZOID TRACKING DEVICE!
THEY *DON'T* NEED TO KNOW EVERYTHING!
SORRY FALA.
C'MON! STOP PLAYING FOR TIME!!
GRG!

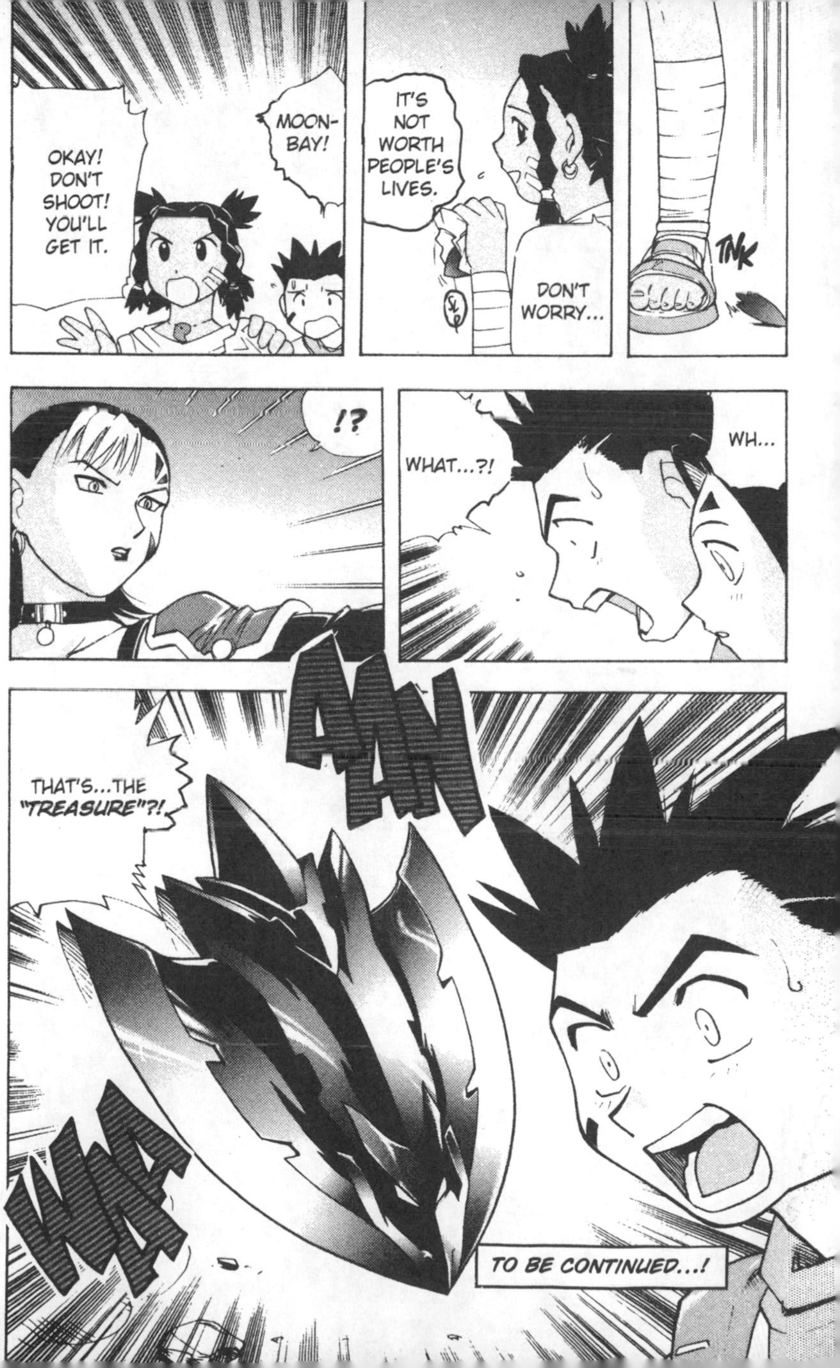
OKAY! DON'T SHOOT! YOU'LL GET IT.
MOON-BAY!
IT'S NOT WORTH PEOPLE'S LIVES.
DON'T WORRY...
TNK
!?
WHAT...?!
WH...
THAT'S...THE *"TREASURE"*?!
TO BE CONTINUED...!

AVAILABLE FROM  VIZ COMICS™
IN NOVEMBER!

Gundam Wing: Blind Target takes place after the TV series and before Endless Waltz. Heero, Wufei, Duo, Trowa, Quatre and Relena are determined to keep peace in the midst of a terrifying plot by a group who wishes to obtain the Gundams for their own dubious ends.

By Akemi Omode
Art by Sakura Asagi
Graphic Novel
b&w, 152 pages
$12.95 USA/$20.95 CAN

Gundam Wing: Episode Zero takes a look at the G Boys' and Relena's origins before Operation Meteor. In Gundam Wing: Episode #8, the latest installment, gain some insight into what events helped shape and influence the personalities and drive for each member of the Gundam team.

By Katsuyuki Sumisawa
Art by Akira Kanbe
monthly comic
b&w, 32 pages
$2.95 USA/$4.95 CAN

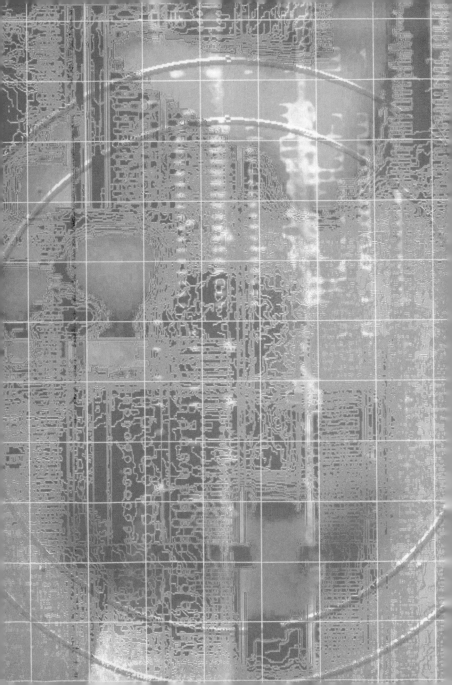